The
Spice
Healer

How a Curry and 73 Other Foods Could Keep You off Prescription Drugs

BY RAY COLLINS
AUTHOR OF *THE LEMON BOOK*

The Spice Healer
How a Curry and 73 Other Foods
Could Keep You off Perscription Drugs

Ray Collins

Copyright © 2009 Fortis Publications Ltd
Published 2009 by Fortis Publications Ltd

www.fortispublications.com

Fortis Publications
Unit 1D, Cherwell Business Village
Southam Road
Banbury, Oxfordshire
OX16 2SP

ISBN: 978-0-9957324-4-7

IMPORTANT NOTE

The publishers have carefully checked the contents of **The Spice Healer** to ensure that it is as accurate as possible at the time of publication.

This book is here to show people the many ways food can be used to treat ailments and protect against disease. Please be advised that the information in these pages is not necessarily representative of the views of health professionals and physicians. Do not treat this as a substitute for medical advice from qualified doctors.

If you are pregnant, we advise that you seek professional advice before you make any dietary changes.

In the case of any emergency, such as an accident, high fever or heart attack, please seek medical attention immediately. If you are worried that you may have a serious illness, please consult a medical professional before trying any of these home remedies.

Neither the author nor the publishers can accept legal responsibility for any problems that may occur when trying the ideas, tips and recipes in this book.

Contents

Editor's Foreword

Ray Collins is the author of *The Lemon Book* and *The Honey Garlic and Vinegar Miracle*. Both are available now at our bookshop on **www.fortispublications.com**

If you enjoy this book you'll also love *The Good Life Letter*, Ray's twice-weekly newsletter. In each issue he reveals natural ways to protect yourself from disease, recover quickly from illness, and ease chronic pain.

Ray doesn't pull any punches. He's honest and open about what he believes works, and what doesn't. And he's not afraid to say what he thinks about the latest health scare stories in the media.

You'll hear about natural remedies from around the world, tasty foods that prevent disease, and breakthrough therapies for ailments most doctors write off as 'incurable'.

Here are some of the gems Ray has uncovered in the past:

- How nuts could help you lose weight, fight depression and heart disease, and even lower your levels of bad cholesterol.

- Why putting dill in your dinner could help relieve your irritable bowel syndrome.

- The Japanese diet secret that could help lower the chance of developing prostate disease.

- Why coffee could cure the morning blues and even boost your memory.

- The amazing Chinese mineral lamp that many people believe can relieve the symptoms of joint and muscle pain, stress and skin conditions.

- How chilli peppers, cherries and peppermint could help relieve back pain.

- The amazing chest-relief remedy discovered in an ancient Transylvanian mine.

Ray also passes on useful tips and advice from his readers. This gives you a remarkable insight into how ordinary people overcome pain, illness and depression.

Subscription to **The Good Life Letter** is absolutely free of charge. To join up, go to www.goodlifeletter.com and enter your email address. (We take your email privacy very seriously and will not pass your details to anyone else.)

For more information on the publisher, please go to our website at www.fortispublications.com. There you can browse our full range of health, money and lifestyle titles.

I hope you enjoy *The Spice Healer.*

Gareth Rees
Editor

How a Yellow Spice Could Challenge the Drug Monopoly

In this book I'm going to talk about *drugs* and *curry*, among many other things. Yes, this is a strange thing for a health commentator to write about. And I'll admit that on the surface of it these two topics could attract *the wrong sort of reader.*

So before I become an unlikely icon for students and college drop-outs I'll quickly explain myself.

Drugs... This book is about the prescription drugs peddled to the nation by major pharmaceutical corporations. These have an important role to play in modern medicine, but they can create as many problems as they solve. And because of a major bias in the media and government towards these drugs and the companies who make them, ordinary people are led to believe they are the only answer.

Many of the prescription drugs mentioned in this book can cause horrible side-effects: vomiting, bleeding, headaches, fatigue, mood swings, among others. If you've ever been through this, or know someone who is on statins, beta blockers, pain killers or HRT drugs, you'll know this very well already.

The medicines can not only make us ill, they often cover up the *symptom* of the problem and don't tackle the *cause*. They're an easy and convenient way for the government to put a sticking plaster over the deeply serious health problems of our time: strokes, heart attacks, high blood pressure, cancer, diabetes and arthritis.

Pharmaceutical companies rely on people to keep taking these drugs, and more of them, so they're hardly motivated to researching the root cause of the problem. They don't spend their research money on finding ways to eliminate the illness for good, certainly not if the answer involves unpatented, natural foods that don't make them a fat profit.

In some cases, their drugs are pushed towards us when we don't really need them at all. And while millions suffer debilitating side effects, very little money is spent on educating the public about ways to prevent serious illness in the first place. My hope is that this book will help you take a stand against this monopoly of vested interests.

Curry... This book is also about curry. By that I don't mean the Saturday night, boozy sing-a-long, vindaloo fests. I refer instead to delicious, healthy home made Asian and Indian food packed full of super-healing spices. You don't even have to like curry to benefit from this. Chapter 1 is all about a very specific and mild spice, one that won't set your tongue on fire.

And it's not just spices that can heal you. I'll also be looking at all kinds of natural ingredients that can protect your health, from garlic, honey and ginger, to tomatoes, fish, mussels and dandelions.

As you'll discover, it's ordinary foods that offer some of the most powerful solutions to the health problems of our time. They can help ease pain, fight infection, recover from illness, prevent major disease and help solve ailments like impotence, hormone imbalances and low libido and energy. In some cases that you'll read about, they even *outperform* the pharmaceuticals.

How I discovered these forgotten food cures

My investigations were inspired by the latest research into the spice turmeric, found in many Asian and Indian dishes. As you'll discover, the main ingredient in this spice can have hugely beneficial effects for people with Alzheimer's, some types of cancer and painful inflammatory diseases. While turmeric is a well-known Indian folk medicine, this is no old wives' tale. Even serious, sceptical scientists are now sitting up and taking notice.

It was when I realised that a curry could prevent disease that I began to write this book. After all, if curry could do this, then what other culinary health miracles were out there? How many other 'forgotten' food remedies are right under our noses?

Before long I had gathered a huge list of natural alternatives to mainstream drugs. Spices, vegetables, garden weeds - and even homemade pizza. They're all remarkably cheap, accessible and tasty. This book will even give you the recipes. And the only side effect is that you'll become a better cook and a more adventurous eater.

I will show you how a Peruvian cabbage can outgun Viagra, how a seafood feast can ease joint pain, how a pizza can protect you from skin cancer, how sage and tofu could help you through the menopause, a soup that helps you sleep, the purple salad that super-charges your energy.

Exciting ways to eat your way to good health

But before you dive in, let me make one thing clear. This is not a manifesto for 'natural vs. artificial'. I'm not a dogmatic, partisan guy looking to slam pharmaceuticals to push an alternative health agenda.

I'm just an ordinary bloke trying to protect my family's health. I believe that conventional medicines have their place. And that you should talk to a health professional if you're worried about a medical problem.

My aim in this book is to offer you natural preventatives, recipes and ideas you can think about as an alternative to mainstream medicine. I want to show you ways you can avoid horrible side effects, and cure little health niggles that don't even need drugs in the first place. By all means take these ideas to your doctor. Research them further. See how they can help you in your daily life.

And yes, hopefully, this book will redress some of the bias in the mainstream media. Open any newspaper these days and you'll see yet another article slamming alternative medicine. Our right to seek out inexpensive, natural cures is constantly under attack.

There are legions of naysayers who dislike alternative health and natural therapies. They especially *love* to hate natural remedies. Many claim that vitamin tablets are 'useless', that taking extra minerals to boost your health is a 'waste of money'.

Almost every week there's another article in the press questioning vitamins and deriding naturopaths as quacks. And shock-horror, almost as many articles in the papers are happy to trumpet the latest 'drug breakthrough'. It's as if an artificial supplement is automatically superior to a natural one.

The tasty food that works like a heart drug

I'll give you an example of why this is very often not the case. At the end of 2008 a study about garlic was reported in the scientific journal *BMC Cardiovascular Disorders*. Dr Reid and her research team discovered that "Garlic may lower blood pressure just as effectively as drugs".

The report revealed that garlic achieved similar effects to those you'd get from well-known anti-hypertensive drugs such as beta blockers and ACE inhibitors. Both of these come with some equally well-known side effects, including fatigue, cold hands and dizziness.

Or here's another recent example. On the 8th of October, *The Daily Mail* ran with this headline: ***"Kitchen honey better at healing burns than standard NHS treatments, say scientists"***.

A group of scientists gathered data from 19 trials involving more than 2,500 patients with a range of wounds. They found that honey was better at reducing recovery time for mild to moderate burns than NHS dressings.

These are classic modern examples of where a common food is found to be as effective as expensive mainstream medicines. And as you'll see in this book, there are plenty more examples.

The Great Drug Swindle

In my view, the attempt to stamp out debate about natural alternatives to conventional treatments is part of a Great Drug Swindle. We are pushed into taking painkillers, antibiotics, depression drugs, sedatives and heart drugs as if they were the only solution. Big corporations get away with peddling sometimes dangerous drugs and medicines that turn out to have terrible side effects, or at times don't even work.

They have press officers, journalists, dedicated laboratories, and doctors on their payroll. They spend millions working to present their expensive drug in the best possible light. Not a problem for them, as they reap billions in rewards for their efforts.

And so we're sold the dream of the miracle wonder pill-man's singular triumph over disease and ill health. Testimony to the human brain's ability to bend or *reverse* the laws of nature! But every invention has a side effect. Many medications utilise chemicals that can cause side effects. Some are minor physical effects, such as nausea or blurred vision. Others affect your mood and emotions.

To give you another example, in October 2008 safety chiefs withdrew a weight loss drug called *Acomplia*. Their concern was that this slimming 'wonder pill' was linked to suicide and sudden death. A report in *The Lancet* found there was a 40% higher chance of being harmed by "adverse events or serious adverse events".

These include a persistently low mood, depression, anxiety, irritability, nervousness and sleep disorders. According to UK health officials, the risk of these side effects "outweighed its benefits".

You don't say!

I don't think any amount of weight loss is worth that kind of misery. And this is the problem with concocting new pharmaceutical drugs in the laboratory.

Why nature's medicine chest is yours to explore

Many people who struggle to improve their health are led towards these medications *by the health professionals they trust*. But instead of a quick cure, people can end up in a fog of confusion, depression and insomnia.

On the other hand, natural medicines, which don't get the laboratory time and can't be patented and sold at a profit, are slammed at every opportunity.

These ideas and foodstuffs have been around for millennia. A lot longer than Western science has been around. Whether we like it or not, millions of people use alternative therapies. They rely on them and benefit from them. So why shouldn't we have access to the information that's available? Why shouldn't we look into these ideas, and find out more about them?

Whatever the scientists think, and whatever the big corporations want us to believe, alternative health practices and practitioners *exist*. People use them and their methods. And they feel better because of it.

You can't pretend they're not there, or declaim everything they ever say as wrong.

It would be terrible if, in the process of denouncing an entire field of therapy, we ignored an avenue of investigation that really could save lives and transform our understanding of medicine.

Whatever your view, I hope you enjoy my book, and find something within these pages that could significantly improve your life.

CHAPTER 1

The Curry that Kills Pain, Fights Cancer & Protects You from Dementia

In my old rugby-playing days it was a macho thing to go out for an Indian meal and order the hottest curry on the menu. With my tongue on fire, I'd wash it down with stupid amounts of beer.

It seemed a good idea at the time, but I'd inevitably spend the next day weeping on the toilet. I may be a big, middle-aged bloke, but when my rear end is on fire, I can cry like a little girl.

These days my tastes are more sophisticated. Firstly, because I've realised that Indian food is a rich and varied landscape of complex flavours and textures, and not some kind of *It's A Knockout* challenge for idiots. Secondly, because of my research into natural remedies, I am now a champion of Indian food as a *health* food.

One reason is that a principle ingredient in Indian food has been shown to help protect you from arthritis, cancer, dementia and Alzheimer's disease.

Why the yellow colour of rice, chutney and curry is so important

One of the principal spices in Indian and Asian food is called turmeric. It gives the dish a vibrant yellow colour, and is used in curries, dhal, pilaf and chutney. The key component of turmeric is called 'curcumin'. This is a powerful little substance which boasts antioxidant, anti-inflammatory and anti-amyloid properties.

- Antioxidants help the body fight the free radicals that cause cancer.

- Anti-inflammatories ease the pain in sore joints and muscles.

- Anti-amyloids stop the production of beta-amyloid, a protein in your brain that many experts now believe is linked to Alzheimer's disease.

Turmeric was already well known in traditional Indian medicine. Ayurvedic practitioners had used it as a medicine for thousands of years. They prescribed it as a natural anti-inflammatory remedy for conditions like flatulence, jaundice, period pain, toothache, and chest pain. Cold and flu sufferers would take a teaspoon of turmeric powder in a cup of warm milk three times every day.

But Western science's exploration of curcumin began only in the 1990s when scientists discovered that the rates of colon, breast, prostate and lung cancer were 15 times *lower* in India than in the United States.

Meanwhile, Americans were four times *more* likely than Indians to develop Alzheimer's. They had a hunch that the high levels of curcumin in the Indian diet could hold the key.

No surprise then that in recent years over 800 studies have been carried out into curcumin and its potential benefits-especially for arthritis, cancer and dementia.

NEW results about curcumin's link to Alzheimer's

Many scientists believe that one of the main causes of Alzheimer's could be a fault in the way beta-amyloid is produced and how your body gets rid of it. These days, scientists are developing artificial drugs that could block or control the production of this protein.

But as usual, it's nature's own medicine chest that could hold the answer. In July 2009 an amazing study was published in the *Journal of Alzheimer's Disease*. It revealed how scientists had discovered that a chemical found in curcumin helped stimulate the immune system to rid the brain of amyloid beta.

Along with a form of vitamin D, called 'vitamin D3', this could offer significant protection against dementia.

But this isn't just an idea that could help us all in the future after further tests. Some experts believe that adding curcumin to your diet **now** is a step in the right direction. This year, Murali Doraiswamy of Duke University, North Carolina, claimed that eating a spicy Indian curry once or twice a week "could help prevent the onset of Alzheimer's disease and dementia".

How curcumin could help fight cancer

Curcumin boasts another amazing quality. It can tell damaged cells to self-destruct so they won't keep multiplying. This process is known as 'apoptosis'. It doesn't work on all forms of cancer, but the effect of curcumin has been successfully tested on the following:

- **Human head and neck squamous cell carcinoma (HNSCC):** curcumin slowed the growth of tumour cells.

- **Mouth cancer:** When applied to the patient's mouth, curcumin stopped the growth of oral cancers.

- **Hepatic cancer:** curcumin decreased the growth of tumours in animal studies.

- **Mantle cell lymphoma:** These tumour cells didn't spread as quickly or greatly when treated with active curcumin.

- **Colon cancer and polyps:** In rodents the curcumin stopped polyps forming. And according to a study published in *Clinical Gastroenterology and Hepatology* in 2006, curcumin and quercitin (an antioxidant in onions) can reduce the number of pre-cancerous lesions in the intestinal tract.

As I mentioned earlier, prostate cancer is rare in India. Some people now believe it's not only the curcumin in the diet, but also the large volume of cruciferous vegetables they consume. These include cauliflower, cabbage, broccoli, kale, and kohlrabi.

Cruciferous vegetables contain chemicals called phenethyl isothiocyanates. In some tests when phenethyl isothiocyanate and curcumin are combined they have helped slow the growth of human prostate cancer cells when implanted in lab mice. Together, these two compounds are more effective than when tested singly. They didn't only slow growth, they also *stopped the spread of the cancer.*

This makes the cauliflower and turmeric dish at the end of this chapter an essential dish for men to try if they want to help boost their protection against prostate cancer.

In July 2009, there was good news for women, too. Researchers at the University of Missouri found that curcumin could reduce the risk of breast cancer in women who have Hormone Replacement Therapy (HRT).

The problem with HRT is that the hormone progestin can increase the levels of something called 'vascular endothelial growth factor' or 'VEGF'. This can speed up the production of certain types of tumour. However, curcumin **prevents** the production of VEGF. This could slow or even stop those breast cancer cells multiplying.

And, amazingly, that wasn't the only bit of publicity regarding curcumin in July 2009.

Time magazine on curcumin as an anti-inflammatory

Time magazine ran an article by Dr. Scott Haig. He explained that the normal anti-inflammatory medications hadn't worked on one of his patients, who was recovering from painful hip replacement surgery. So instead, he gave him turmeric capsules.

He reported: *"Soon enough, there was no pain at all. And his lower back and hands, which ached before, were also now pain-free."*

Now, the conventional medicinal route for inflammatory problems like arthritis is to offer you COX-2 inhibitors.

Two of the most popular, called valdecoxib (Bextra) and rofecoxib (Vioxx) were taken off the UK market because of their side effects - including stomach, vascular and heart problems. However, in the UK you can still be prescribed celecoxib (Celebrex) and etoricoxib (Arcoxia).

Curcumin could be a serious alternative to these drugs. It has also been shown to inhibit the COX-2 enzyme without any of the horrible side effects. It also inhibits something called the 'nuclear factor kappa beta', another substance involved in inflammation.

One trial in humans with rheumatoid arthritis found that curcumin offered sufferers a significant improvement in morning stiffness, walking time, and levels of swelling.

How much curcumin do you need to reap the benefits?

Estimates say that the daily intake of turmeric in the Indian diet is about 2-2.5g. This is equal to about 60-100mg of curcumin each day. Most studies quoted in this book used 1,200mg of 95% standardized curcumin as a very strong medicinal dose. But many capsules I've seen on sale as a health supplement hold 500mg in each.

But the best advice of all is simply to eat a good, homemade curry once every week with plenty of turmeric in it. I can't think of a better, healthier, tastier way to reinforce your body's natural defences against serious disease.

However, beware that curcumin increases your body's production of bile. This isn't a problem, but it makes it one to avoid for pregnant women and anyone with gallstones.

Turmeric is just one of the principal ingredients of spicy Asian and India food that has such powerful benefits. But there are two more I'd like to mention in this chapter.

The food that stops a heart attack

Cayenne pepper, or capsicum, is widely used in spicy dishes. This herb has the power to increase blood circulation and stimulate the heart. In fact, it has been shown to stop a heart attack within 30 seconds. Get hold of some cayenne pepper and keep it handy in case of an emergency.

If you are waiting for the ambulance in the event of a suspected heart attack, put a teaspoon into a cup of warm water, and drink immediately. And if you are giving someone CPR and can't administer the cayenne in warm water, drop some cayenne extract into the mouth.

You can also apply cayenne pepper directly onto wounds to stop the bleeding. It does this by regulating the body's blood pressure so that the pressure at the wound area is lessened.

Another spice that eases pain

Ginger is another spicy food remedy you may have hanging about the home. It's not just a good way to spice up cakes, biscuits and cups of chocolate. It's actually a very potent natural remedy for a whole host of ailments.

For example, in a 1992 study, ginger was given to people suffering from muscle pain. An encouraging 75% of the test subjects with rheumatoid arthritis or osteoarthritis said they felt substantial relief.

If you've got inflamed joints, try drinking fresh ginger juice, extract, or tea every day. Take no more than 2 to 4gs daily. To make the tea you need to:

- Slice a two-inch chunk of fresh ginger root into very thin slices.

- Boil four cups worth of water.

- Stew the ginger and water in a teapot or on a covered pot on the hob for 15 minutes.

- Strain and serve.

- Add honey and/or lemon to enhance the taste.

For a quicker method, grate three teaspoons of ginger to a cup of boiling water.

You can also use ginger as a topical agent by rubbing ginger oil directly into the painful joint. Or take some fresh ginger root, put it in a compress and then apply it.

Try seeking out an essential oil made from ginger. You can use this oil in massages to treat rheumatism, lumbago, or for bone injuries. It also combines well with almond oil, juniper or eucalyptus oils.

Quick and Easy Dal (Indian Lentils)

Ingredients:
2 medium onions, finely diced
2 cloves garlic, minced
1/2 teaspoon fresh ginger root, finely grated
2 Tbsp extra virgin olive oil
2 x 400g tins of lentils
1/2 teaspoon turmeric
1/2 teaspoon ground cumin
1/4 teaspoon sea salt, or to taste
1/4 teaspoon freshly ground black pepper
1 1/2 teaspoons lemon juice, freshly squeezed
30g fresh parsley, chopped

Method:
Mince one onion and the garlic. Heat one tablespoon of olive oil in a saucepan. Sauté the onion, garlic and ginger. Add the lentils, turmeric, cumin, pepper and sea salt. Cover and cook for 10 minutes. Turn off the flame and mix in the lemon juice and half the parsley.

Slice the remaining onion. Sauté the onion in remaining tablespoon of oil until golden and translucent.

Place the lentils in a serving bowl. Garnish with remaining parsley and sautéed onions. Serve.

As a variation, one cup of cooked organic basmati rice or barley may be cooked with the lentils.

Recipe courtesy of Eden Foods,
www.edenfoods.com

Chicken Curry (Pressure Cooker Recipe)

Serves: 4

Ingredients:
200g brown rice
1 tbsp. olive, coconut or canola oil
450g chicken breasts cut into 3/4" pieces
4 large onions cut into wedges
11/4 cups water
4 garlic cloves, minced
1 tsp peanut oil
1 tbsp soy sauce
1 tsp chilli powder
1 tsp curry powder
11/4 tsp turmeric
1 tsp ground ginger
2 tbsp fresh coriander, chopped

Method:
Cook rice using pot in pot method* and set aside in a warm place.

In the pressure cooker, heat oil and sauté chicken and onions over medium-high heat until chicken is lightly browned. Add water, garlic, oil, and soy sauce; then add chili powder, curry, turmeric and ground ginger and stir till well blended.

Lock the lid in place and bring to pressure. Lower heat and cook for 4 minutes at 15psi. Allow pressure to drop by the natural release method for 4 minutes, then release the remaining pressure using the quick release method or automatic release method and remove lid.

Stir in coriander and serve over warm rice.

The pot-in-pot method is a quick and easy way of cooking rice without it sticking to the pressure cooker. You'll need a heat-proof pot (or bowl) that fits inside your pressure cooker. A stainless steel one is a good choice. Pour 1 cup (250 ml) of water into the bottom of the pressure cooker. Place the trivet in the pressure cooker and, if necessary to support the stainless steel pot, the steamer basket. The stainless steel pot/bowl is now put on top of the trivet or steamer basket. You can add various seasonings to the rice (garlic, basil, thyme, cayenne.) 1 cup of brown rice will take 5-7 minutes to cook.

Recipe courtesy of Natural Mom's Recipes,
www.naturalmomsrecipes.com

Indian Coconut Shrimp

Serves: 4 as a side dish

Ingredients:
1 small coconut, drained and the meat grated
  (to simplify you can buy unsweetened flaked coconut)
350g prawns, peeled and deveined
1 onion, chopped
1/2 tsp ground turmeric
1 tsp ground cayenne pepper (or less if you don't like it too spicy)
3 tbsp coconut or olive oil
1 tsp salt

Method:
Heat the vegetable oil in a large skillet. Add the onion and sauté until translucent.

Add the shredded coconut and continue to sauté for another few minutes. Add the turmeric, pepper and salt and mix well.

Then add the prawns (and if you like it a bit juicier you can add a bit of water). Cook for about 15 minutes on low heat.

Serve immediately with rice or other Indian dishes.

Recipe courtesy of Natural Mom's Recipes,
www.naturalmomsrecipes.com

Vegetarian Thai Curry with Greens

Serves: 4

Ingredients:
Splash of coconut oil
1 can coconut milk
3 courgettes, thickly sliced
200g fresh peas
200g asparagus, cut in 4 cm pieces
10 fresh basil leaves

For the curry paste:
5 Thai chillies, deseeded if you don't like it too hot!
1 tsp cumin
1 tsp coriander seeds
2 shallots, roughly chopped
4 cm ginger root, grated
2 garlic cloves, roughly chopped
2 lemongrass stalks, roughly chopped
Zest of 1 lime, finely grated
1/4 tsp turmeric
1/2 tbsp palm sugar (also called jaggery, you can find it at some natural grocers or Asian markets)
A handful of fresh coriander, plus extra to serve
Black pepper
Pepper and salt to season
Splash of coconut oil

Method:

To make the paste, dry-fry all the spices and then grind them in a mortar and pestle. Put the mixture into a blender and add all the remaining paste ingredients. Blend for about 5 minutes or until smooth and set aside.

In a large frying pan, heat the oil over low heat, add about 3 tbsp of the curry paste. Stir and cook for about 2 minutes, then add the coconut milk. Bring to a boil and simmer for 5 minutes.

In the meantime, coat the courgette slices with oil, season with salt and pepper, and fry on a hot griddle pan for 2 minutes each side.

Add the grilled courgette slices to the curry and cook for about 5 minutes.

Add the asparagus and peas and cook for a further 3 - 4 minutes.

Stir in the basil leaves and serve immediately with jasmine rice and lime wedges.

Enjoy!

Recipe courtesy of Natural Mom's Recipes,
www.naturalmomsrecipes.com

Cauliflower with Turmeric - Two Ways

Ingredients:
A large cauliflower, cut into florets
500 ml of vegetable stock
1 tsp turmeric
extra virgin olive oil
Half a lemon
1 tbsp grated fresh ginger (optional)
salt and pepper

First method:
Bring the stock to the boil in a pot, then turn the heat down so it's simmering.

Cut the florets into quarters and add them to the pot with the turmeric. Put a lid on the pot. Cook for 5 minutes. Drain excess water. Drizzle with olive oil and season well.

Second method:
Mix the cauliflower florets with 3 tablespoons of olive oil, a teaspoon of turmeric and then season well. For an extra kick, add a tablespoon of grated ginger. Place the mix in a casserole dish and roast in the oven at 180 degrees until golden brown. Squeeze some lemon juice afterwards and then serve.

CHAPTER 2

The Seafood that Prevents Heart Attacks and Eases Joint Pain

Back in the 1970s, while studying the Greenland Inuit, Danish scientists noticed a strange phenomenon. The Inuit had a very low incidence of inflammatory diseases such as asthma, rheumatoid arthritis, diabetes and psoriasis. Along with this, they were pretty much free from heart disease.

And yet their diet was chocka full of fat… their meals consisting almost entirely of whale meat, seal blubber and salmon. How could this be?

The secret was in the large amounts of omega-3 fats in the food they ate. Yes, FAT! The enemy of all dieters since time began. The blame for all the evils of the world!

How these 'good fats' help your heart

Omega-3 fatty acids are converted in the body into natural anti-inflammatory substances known as prostaglandins and leukotrienes. This is why the Inuit were less prone to inflammatory diseases, and why doctors in Dundee are now excited about the potential for treating rheumatoid arthritis.

Omega-3 fats are shown to reduce levels of triglycerides. This is the sort of fat found in the blood that has been linked to heart disease.

Recently, an Italian study published in *The Lancet* showed that fish oils given to more than 4,000 patients after a heart attack helped to prevent a secondary event. Now the Italian health service gives out fish-oil capsules to everyone who has a heart attack!

How to get your omega 3s

The best way to get omega 3s into your body is to eat oily fish twice a week. These include: sardines, herring, mackerel, trout, salmon, kippers, fresh tuna and anchovies. Try the fish recipe at the end of this chapter. Try the fish curry with turmeric at the end of this chapter to get all the anti-inflammatory benefits of this wonderful spice (see Chapter 1 for more on this.)

You can also use good quality cod liver oil tablets or other fish oils. Go for supplements that include small amounts of vitamin E. This protects the oil from being damaged by free radicals in your body before it can work its magic.

What's exciting is that intelligent and open-minded mainstream GPs are using this as part of their approach to illness. Glasgow GP Dr. Tom Gilhooly, who also runs the Essential Health Clinic, says:

"Working with patients to increase their omega-3 levels can help to treat conditions as varied as MS, depression, drug addiction and Crohn's disease."

So let me get this right. This is a case of natural medicine being used by a renowned doctor as part of a holistic approach to the diseases of modern times? Well I never! There's hope for us all.

But there's another type of food that trumps fish for its abilities to lower inflammation. It's a delicious and rare type of seafood…

Why blue whales get so big, and why it matters to you

Jacques Cousteau, the undersea explorer, once said, "The future of nutrition is found in the ocean". You don't need to tell *that* to the Maoris of New Zealand. Thanks to the powerful phytoplankton in the seas around them, they've lived mercifully free of most arthritis-related diseases.

Phytoplankton are tiny organisms which drift near the surface of the sea. They turn sunlight, water and minerals into protein, carbohydrates, vitamins and amino acids. They're a building block of life, and responsible for 90% of the Earth's oxygen.

Plankton is the principal diet of blue whales and humpback whales. So considering how big these beasts grow, it's obvious that plankton packs a SERIOUS nutritional punch.

In New Zealand, this phytoplankton is particularly special. It's one of those spots on the planet where extreme conditions have combined to create a breed of super plankton. The sunshine that hits the New Zealand coastline is so intense that, over millions of years, these plankton have developed the most complex and powerful set of antioxidants found anywhere in nature.

But the Maoris don't eat the plankton itself. Certainly not. And you won't find me about to bite into a plankton sandwich either.

No. For centuries the Maoris have feasted on the delicious green-lipped mussels which feed on that plankton. These plankton-rich mussels produce something called 'lipid oil'. As scientists have discovered, this is a powerful anti-inflammatory. And it's *this* aspect of New Zealand's green-lipped mussels which gives people protection from joint pain.

The easy way to benefit from green-lipped mussels

I wish the answer was as simple as eating ordinary mussels from your fishmonger.

Although, saying that, there ARE benefits of doings such a thing.

Ordinary mussels provide easily absorbed doses of vitamins B and C, plus amino acids, Omega-3 fatty acids, iron, manganese, phosphorus, potassium, selenium and zinc. And they have a very low glycemic index (GI) which makes them a great diet food. They fill you up without giving you that carbohydrate rush and crash.

But when it comes to easing joint pain and asthma, you really need to try the New Zealand green-lipped mussels. And the easiest way is to take a supplement. One of the versions on the market right now is called Lyprinol. This is an extract of green-lipped mussels. It contains those all-important lipid groups, plus omega-3 polyunsaturated fatty acids - the good fats that help your heart.

Ray's Mussels in White Wine

Serves: 4

Ingredients:
1 tbsp extra virgin olive oil
1 tbsp butter
4 cloves chopped garlic
A medium onion (sliced)
A bay leaf
A cup of white wine
4lb mussels, cleaned
Fresh cream (optional)
Handful of chopped parsley
Salt and black pepper

Method:
Take a large pot and shallow-fry the onion in olive oil and butter over a low heat. Keep going until the onion is translucent and soft. Add the chopped garlic and continue for a few more minutes (add the garlic too early and it will burn and taste bitter).

Now add the mussels, bay leaf and wine. Add salt and pepper. Turn the heat up really high and put a lid on the pot. As the mussels start to steam, give the pot an occasional shake. Wait for the mussels to open. This takes about 2-8 minutes. Discard any mussels that don't open.

Now pour in the cream if using and parsley, and stir. Taste and add more seasoning if you like.

Remove the bay leaf and serve with crusty brown bread.

Easy Mackerel For Two

Ingredients:
2 whole mackerel, gutted and scaled.
1 tbsp virgin olive oil
3 cloves garlic
A lemon
2 shallots, chopped
Chopped parsley
Two large sprigs of rosemary
Quarter glass of white wine
Salt and Pepper

Method:
Rub the fish with oil and place on baking paper in a dish with raised edges.

Season inside and out with salt and pepper.

Place a rosemary sprig inside each fish.

Place a slice of lemon on each side of the fish.

Pour a tablespoon of white wine over each fish.

Sprinkle some chopped shallots and parsley over the fish.

Wrap up the fish and bake the two parcels on a tray for 20 minutes at 180°C (test with a knife to check if it's done properly).

Fish Curry

Ingredients

30g butter
2 teaspoons of turmeric
A teaspoon of cumin
A tablespoon of ground coriander
A tablespoon of fennel seed
A teaspoon of garam masala
Parsley, finely chopped
Coriander, finely chopped
1cm piece of fresh ginger
A chopped 1 onion
A clove of garlic, chopped
200ml milk
50g creamed coconut
450g of firm white fish, like Pollock or cod, cut into chunks.

method

Fry the onion in the pan, with the garlic and ginger for 5 minutes, until the onion becomes translucent. Mix the cumin, turmeric, ground coriander, and fennel seed with a spoon of vinegar until it creates a paste. Add this to the pan. Cook for another 5 minutes.

Warm the milk in a pot and stir in the coconut until dissolved. Now add this to the pan and bring to the boil.

Now bring it all down to a simmer and add the fish, parsley and chopped coriander and cook for 10 minutes or until the fish is firm.

CHAPTER 3

The Pizza that Could Help Protect You from Asthma & Skin Cancer

In a unique trial in 2007, a research team at the Hunter Medical Research Institute in Australia fed a group of asthmatics a diet rich in lycopene. This is an antioxidant found in tomatoes and especially tomato sauce, paste and juice. For instance, the sauce you get on a good pizza is absolutely packed with this type of antioxidant.

A pizza! Who'd have thought it?

During the trial at the Hunter Medical Research Institute, one group of subjects drank three glasses of tomato juice each day. The others swallowed tomato extract in capsules.

Dr Lisa Wood, who led the research, said both groups showed improvements in airway inflammation. And in January 2006, another study had equally amazing implications.

Why smokers should drink tomato juice

Japanese researchers showed that drinking tomato juice completely prevented emphysema in mice which had been exposed to tobacco smoke. They even went so far as to suggest that smokers and non-smokers exposed to second-hand smoke should drink tomato juice every day.

This backs up a 2002 study from Finland, reported in the *American Journal of Epidemiology*. Researchers on that project found these results after testing male smokers aged 37 to 69:

- A high fruit and vegetable intake reduced their risk of lung cancer by 27%.

- A higher intake of lycopene reduced their risk by 28%.

- The foods that produced the greatest reduction in lung cancer risk were tomatoes and especially tomato paste and sauces, which are the best sources of lycopene.

And that's not the only benefits of eating a rich, red tomato paste. It could be a far better weapon in the fight against skin cancer than suntan lotion.

Why suntan lotion can be bad for you

Drs. Cedric and Frank Garland of the University of California claim that although sunscreen can protect against sunburn, there's no proof that they protect against melanoma. They even claim that by blocking

UV light from the sun, it prevents your body producing its own vitamin D.

This vitamin is vital, because according to the website *Natural News*, studies show that vitamin D "prevents up to 77 of ALL cancers in women (breast cancer, colon cancer, cervical cancer, lung cancer, brain tumours, multiple myeloma.)"

There are three further sources I've found that suggest a potential health problem with suntan lotions:

1. **Scientists at the Swiss National Research programme** have warned that 'endocrine disrupters' in sunscreens could harm both adults and children.

2. **A study by the US Centers for Disease Control (CDC)** claims that 97% of Americans are contaminated with a widely-used sunscreen ingredient called oxybenzone. This has been linked to allergies, hormone disruption and cell damage.

3. **Research by Dr Exley at Keele University published on the 14th of August 2007** suggested that the presence of aluminium salts in sunscreens could be dangerous. In his opinion the pro-oxidant qualities of this metal means it may cause oxidative damage in the skin such as wrinkles, skin ageing and even cancer.

Now, I don't want to scaremonger. I simply want to present a side of the story not told by the big corporations who produce suntan lotion. A safer solution may be to protect your skin from the inside.

Lycopene-a possibility for cancer prevention

At the University of Manchester, they've discovered that test subjects who ate tomato paste were 33% more protected against the sun. This is the equivalent to putting on factor 1.3 suntan lotion.

The boffins reckon it could be something to do with lycopene. This substance neutralises the harmful molecules in your skin when you get too much sun. These molecules are responsible for premature ageing and skin cancer.

Similar tests at the University of Newcastle have shown that lycopene reduces the disruption of mitochondrial DNA in your skin. This 'disruption' has been linked to skin ageing. So this is a potent, natural anti-wrinkle remedy, too.

Why a paste, specifically, and not an ordinary tomato? Well, apparently, the heating process frees up the lycopene. To try out the paste all you need to do is make a healthy homemade pizza.

Vegan Pizza

Ingredients:
For the Pizza Dough
400g organic unbleached white flour
1 package dry yeast
2 tbsp extra virgin olive oil
1/2 teaspoon sea salt
350ml warm water, about 85°F.
Extra virgin olive oil, for oiling the bowl

Toppings:
190g jar of tomato paste
1 small red onion, sliced into thin rings
1 cup button mushrooms, sliced thin
or a variety of fresh mushrooms
1 medium green bell pepper, sliced into thin strips
200g pitted black olives, sliced thin

Directions:
Combine dry yeast, oil and warm water in a small bowl. Stir for several seconds until yeast dissolves. Combine flour and sea salt. Pour wet ingredients into dry ingredients and mix to form a ball of dough. Knead for 10 minutes. Lightly oil a large mixing bowl and place the dough in it. Cover with a damp cloth, place in a warm area and let rise for approximately 2 hours until the dough doubles in size. Divide the dough in half and form 2 pizza crusts. Place the dough on pizza pans and add equal amounts of pizza sauce, onion, mushrooms, green pepper and olives. Allow to rest for 10 minutes.

While the pizzas are resting, preheat the oven to 220°C. Bake the pizzas for 25 to 30 minutes or until the crust is light brown on the bottom and crispy. Slice each pizza into 8 equal size wedges and serve.

Yields: 2 pizza pies; 16 slices

Recipe courtesy of Eden Foods,
www.edenfoods.com

Ray's Pizza Funghi

Ingredients for the dough:
2 tsp of active dry yeast
A cup warm of water
A tsp sugar
2 tbsp of olive oil
250g of organic unbleached flour
A pinch of salt

Ingredients for the topping:
1 can of tomato paste
chopped mushrooms
Sliced onion and/or ham
Plenty of mozzarella cheese
A drizzle of olive oil

Method:
Use the same dough-making technique as recommended in the Vegan pizza recipe.

Add the toppings, add a drizzle of olive oil. Bake at 220°C degrees for 20 minutes

CHAPTER 4

How to Prevent a Blood Clot With Tea and a Jam Sandwich

Estimates say that blood clots kill around 25,000 people in this country every year. That's 20 times the number of people who die from MRSA, the deadly 'dirty hospital' bug that keeps hitting the headlines.

Beverly Hunt, the medical director of Lifeblood (a thrombosis charity) said: "It's nothing short of a public health emergency."

The major problem is that blood clots are not viewed as a primary concern by the authorities. Hospital staff are practically bent double under the weight of work they have. They simply don't have the time to check for the presence of blood clots, even though 25,000 people a year die as a result of this ailment.

Of course, blood clots will take lives even if doctors stopped everything else and gave each patient the best medical care possible. But the number of deaths could fall significantly if more time was dedicated to the problem.

And there's another factor that's making the number scarily high. At present, the drugs used to treat blood clots aren't that reliable. In fact, they can cause additional problems. Is it any wonder, when you see what they're using?

A prescription of rat poison...

Warfarin is a drug that's often used to treat blood clots. You and I know it better as rat poison. Now, I don't care how many spoonfuls of sugar Mary Poppins gave me, this particular medicine would never go down a treat.

Side effects include: severe bleeding; hives; rashes or itching; swelling of the face, throat, mouth, legs, feet or hands; chest pain; vomiting; fever; muscle ache; diarrhoea; numbness.

There's another-more alarming-problem with Warfarin. It may indeed break up the blood clot, but the effect of Warfarin goes too far the other way. In fact, it thins the blood so much that patients can suffer dangerous haemorrhages.

So what can the likes of you and me do to protect against this threat?

Unfortunately, nothing is foolproof. Like I said earlier, blood clots can crop up alarmingly quickly in some people, and no amount of medical care or treatment can help.

But Mother Nature, as always, boasts some remarkable remedies that could offer some potential answers to the blood clot problem:

Ginger tea – The properties of ginger seem to reduce the risk of heart attack by preventing internal blood clots, and the easiest way to get into the routine of taking ginger is to put the kettle on and make some tea. Just add two teaspoons of grated or powdered ginger in a cup of hot water. Let it stand for 10 minutes before you drink. Have up to three cups daily.

Healthy worms – Chinese people have used earthworms for thousands of years in their medicines to invigorate blood circulation, dissolve stasis, open up channels, and cure stroke, hemiplegia and infantile convulsion. And this use is backed up by science, which identified three clot-busting enzymes in the earthworm: fibrinolysin (plasmin), profibrinolysin activator and collagenase.

When taken, these three enzymes work together to beat the clot. The plasmin is attracted to the clot and attaches itself to the surface. The collagenase then breaks down the surface of the clot, leaving the plasmin and the activator to enter the clot and break it down. As the clot dissolves, the blood vessel opens up and the build up of pressure drains away.

Apparently, this treatment is used extensively in China, and with great success – and no side effects. But before you go out searching for earthworm supplements, check this out with your doctor first.

Garlic – Another all round good guy, garlic helps keep the blood thin and active, making it more difficult for clots.

Bilberry – One of my all-time favourite remedies (it can be made into jam, which is far tastier than rat poison in my opinion). Bilberry has so many powerful health benefits: it thins the blood, prevents capillaries from becoming weak, and lowers high blood pressure. If you can't get hold of bilberries, track down a bilberry supplement. And if all else fails, try blueberries instead in the jam recipe I've recommended for you. Eat it with some healthy, homemade wholemeal bead.

And for the perfect, healthy afternoon treat, try ginger tea and a blueberry jam sandwich.

Bilberry (or blueberry) Jam

Ingredients:
3 lb of clean, fresh bilberries
with 1 1/2 lb of sugar

Method:
Because of its richness, the bilberry is the fruit that needs the least amount of sugar when turning it into jam. You require only half a pound of sugar to a pound of berries.

To make bilberry jam, put the fruit in a preserving pan. Add a cupful of water.

Boil for 40 minutes, cool and then store in screw-top jars.

You can try the same with blueberries.

CHAPTER 5

The 'Unhealthy' Drink That Could Protect Your Brain and Eyesight

In the old days, a simple cup of coffee could inspire a clash of emotions. I would mentally lash myself every time I reached for the second pot to keep me going at work. The black stuff was so tasty, so energising, and so ruddy addictive, too. Many decried it as an evil drug. A mind-rotting scourge like crack cocaine or daytime TV. The media told us this. And therefore we felt that it was true.

It's all changed now, though. Just look what they're saying about coffee these days. Emblazoned on the BBC News website on the 5th of July 2009 you could have read the following:

"Drinking five cups of coffee a day could reverse memory problems seen in Alzheimer's disease, US scientists say."

In the labs, mice were given largish amounts of caffeine. Not in big steaming mugs from Costa, I might add, but in 500 mg doses. These mice showed a 50% reduction in their levels of 'beta amyloid protein' (see chapter 1 for more about this). This is yet another significant chapter in the story of coffee.

Far from being a demonic substance, more and more research suggests that a moderate dose of caffeine can have positive effects.

Why the coffee-hating 'do gooders' got it wrong

Over the years, writing about food and health, I've championed a sensible approach to coffee. Partly because I like the stuff. Partly because I think a lot of damage was done by the food scares and fads of the 70s and 80s.

Back then we were pushed into low fat diets and sugar-free foods. These have subsequently been found to be either pointless, or even *dangerous*. Butter was replaced by margarines. This synthetic food is now accused of being high in trans fatty acids. A substance that many critics claim *can triple your risk of coronary heart disease.*

Sugar was replaced by sweeteners like aspartame. Today, this substance stands accused of being linked to 92 health problems including abdominal pain, arthritis, asthma, chronic coughs, chronic fatigue, depression, headaches, heart palpitations, hypertension, impotency, insomnia, irritability, memory loss, muscle spasms, nausea, rashes, tinnitus and blurred vision.

At the same time as these poisons were recommended as the 'healthy alternative', good old-fashioned staples like coffee were replaced by horrible decaffeinated versions.

But since the 90s, the tables have turned.

Could coffee even protect your eyesight?

The caffeine in coffee is now said to lower your risk of diabetes, Parkinson's disease and headaches. Studies have shown that caffeine can improve your attention span and boost brainpower. And a 2007 study, reported in the *Journal of Neurology, Neurosurgery and Psychiatry*, suggests that drinking coffee can even protect your eyesight.

Italian researchers looked at the coffee drinking and smoking habits of 166 people with a condition called 'blepharospasm'. This is where you get an uncontrollable spasm in your eyelid.

It's not just annoying, it can lead to blindness.

Now it's claimed that one or two cups of coffee a day can reduce the risk of this condition.

In January 2007, the *Journal of Pain* suggested that drinking coffee could help reduce the pain you get after exercise.

The study found that two cups of coffee can cut muscle pain by up to 48%. Now I'm not suggesting for a minute that coffee is a new health drink, to be guzzled wantonly throughout the day. Experts say that 200 mg (two cups of coffee) is the optimal dose. But I think that from now on, you can settle back and enjoy your morning cup of coffee without your conscience being tortured.

More delicious ways to protect your eyesight

- Bilberries. I've talked about these little marvels in Chapter 4, and here I go again. Bilberries contain a powerful ingredient called anthocyanosides. These help protect and improve the tiny capillaries that feed the eyes, control inflammation and gently fight any free radicals that wander into this sensitive area.

- Carrot juice. This is packed with Vitamin A - a must for healthy eyes. Try drinking a glass at least twice a week.

- Parsley juice. Rather than acting as a powerful cure-all like carrot juice, parsley juice attacks specific problems like cataracts and conjunctivitis. But beware, parsley juice is pretty potent, so don't guzzle it like a normal drink. Instead try mixing 30ml once a week with your carrot juice.

How to ease tired eyes with a potato

Sometimes it's the little things that matter, and even if your eyes are 20/20, they still need some love and attention from time to time.

Try these tips if you want to refresh them:

- Cut raw potato and place a slice over each eye. Lie back and relax for 15 minutes.

- Mix 1 tbsp of parsley, 1 tbsp of fennel and 1 tbsp of mint in a cup of boiling water. Let it stand for 10-15 minutes. Now dip cotton balls into the 'tea' and place on your eyelids for 10 minutes.

- Fill a bowl with very cold water. Lower your face into the water for 20 seconds (if you're comfortable with that. If not, shorten the time). Lift your face out, have a breather for 30 seconds, then tilt your head and stick your eyes and forehead into the water. Open your eyes for 5 seconds, then pull back. Repeat 5 times.

CHAPTER 6

Herbs that Help You Give Up Smoking

Want to give up smoking? Withdrawal symptoms getting you down? Ladies and Gentlemen, I give you the incredible stop-smoking pill. Just pop this little fella down twice a day and quit smoking the easy way.

In theory, the pill known as *Champix* sounds reasonable. It mimics the effects of nicotine on the body, which dulls cravings and withdrawal symptoms. And if you do cave in to temptation, Champix limits the damage done.

Those are the good points. But as ever, there are bad points…

What comes first… £500 million or your health?

First off, the dreaded side effects. The official line is that side effects include nausea. *Include* nausea. I wonder what the other ones will turn out to be? Secondly, this pill is set to make Pfizer (the drug company behind Champix) £500 million a year. Now call me a cynic, but I just wonder how clear your judgement is when £500 million a year is dangled in front of your nose.

I'm not for a second suggesting that Lord Pfizer stands astride his empire laughing like some pantomime villain as his scientists are lashed by evil trolls to invent more pills (though as you can see I have given it some thought). But what comes first with drugs companies, their profit or your health?

Instead, here are a few natural ways to curb cravings and protect your body from the perils of nicotine.

Natural tips for giving up smoking

Gotu Kola has been used as a medicinal herb for thousands of years in India. It is said to help control the imbalance in your body's chemical make-up that occurs when you have an addiction. Gotu Kola could also dull your sugar cravings, which go through the roof when you pack up smoking. (By the way, Gotu Kola does NOT contain caffeine, unlike the kola nut, which is an active ingredient in the fizzy drink.)

Avena sativa is another traditional Indian herb. For centuries it has been used to treat opium addiction, but recently it's been suggested that this nerve tonic could numb your nicotine cravings by neutralising the imbalance in brain chemicals caused by addiction.

Another herb to look into is ashwagandha. This is considered by many to be one of the most powerful and useful Ayurvedic remedies. It's sometimes called 'The Indian Ginseng'. It improves immunity, and helps your body cope with chemical stresses - which is exactly what it's going through when you give up smoking.

Some naturopaths believe that St. John's wort and the Chinese herb scutellaria can lift depression and ease mood swings.

You could also try magnesium. When you absorb nicotine your brain releases a chemical called dopamine. This is a feel-good chemical. After a while, you get used to this pleasurable release, and want more of it. So you have another cigarette. But by taking magnesium, you can increase your natural levels of dopamine, and take the edge off your cravings.

A tasty way to end your cravings

Smoking strips away your body's nutrients, so you need to pack them back in. Add plenty of fresh vegetables and fruit to your diet. It's tough for your body to clean up when you smoke, so give it a helping hand by removing as many of the pathogens and free radicals as possible. By reducing the toxic load in the body, your immune system has more time to deal with any cancer cells that may be present.

Great detox foods include broccoli, cauliflower, onions, garlic, artichokes, beets, and red and green vegetables. Get hold of as many as possible and make the soup I recommend on the next page.

Ray's Detox Vegetable Soup

Ingredients:
Florets of broccoli
Florets of cauliflower
1 large onion
Chopped leek
Chopped celery
2 cloves garlic
Raw, chopped beetroot
2 potatoes
Finely chopped carrots
Chopped parsley
Thyme (leaves not the stalks)
Vegetable stock

Method:
As you can see there's no specific recipe here. Personally, I like to 'wing it' with soups. I chuck it all in and see what happens. I never make the same soup with the same taste twice, which keeps life for this middle-aged man relatively exciting.

A rough guide to how I do it…

Sweat the onion, leek and celery until soft and translucent. Add the garlic and thyme and cook a bit more.

Now turn up the heat, add in the potato, carrot and beetroot and cook for 2-5 minutes.

Now add the stock, broccoli and cauliflower. Bring to the boil.

Then reduce the heat and simmer until the vegetables are soft. Add more stock if necessary, or keep it going for longer if you want to reduce it more.

Season to taste and add the parsley near the end.

Eat it in its chunky glory, or liquidise it with a hand blender. If you want to be indulgent, add some cream at the end.

CHAPTER 7

A Soup that Helps You Sleep

In 2001 the charity MIND launched a booklet called *Sleeping Pills Curse or Cure for Insomnia?* It warned that withdrawal symptoms can be severe, ranging from trembling and the shakes… to dizziness and loss of balance… to hallucinations, paranoia and epileptic fits.

They also said that anyone who has taken sleeping tablets for more than a few nights shouldn't try withdrawal without the help of their GP. That's how addictive these things are!

Yet up to a third of elderly people in the UK are prescribed sleeping pills because they are affected by insomnia. But do they work in the long run?

Canadian researchers carried out a series of studies on sedative drugs between 1966 and 2003. They concluded that the risk of the side effects such as dizziness, loss of balance, falls, and disorientation far outweighed the benefits of the drugs.

The studies covered a range of medications, including antihistamines and prescription drugs like benzodiazepine. In their studies seven cases of dizziness led to life-threatening incidents... six serious falls and a car crash!

The Canadian researchers conclusion was clear. Older people are more than TWICE as likely to experience an adverse incident after taking sedatives as they are to gain a better quality of sleep.

7 ways to calm your nervous system

- Up your intake of **B vitamins**, especially B6, B3 and B12. They help regulate the body's response to stress and maintain a healthy nervous system.

- **Calcium, magnesium** and **zinc** as well as C supplements can help calm the nervous system and so help treat insomnia.

- **Valerian** is well-known as a natural sleep aid and sedative. Recent trials have found it can work as well as drugs like Valium, without the side effects. (Try and find a standardised extract.)

- Some studies also suggest that **Passion Flower** can lower anxiety that leads to sleeplessness. If you get your hands on a herbal remedy that combines passion flower and valerian extracts, this will be even more effective.

- **Chaste Tree** is a herb that is said to increase your body's natural production of melatonin. This helps you have a more restful sleep.

- **L-theanine**, an amino acid derived from green tea, reduces anxiety. Some people report that it works as well as prescription medications, without being addictive or habit-forming.

- **Seditol** is a branded product that acts as an anti-stress and anti-anxiety formula. But it's made of two entirely natural herbal ingredients, **magnolia** and **ziziphus**. Users have reported that it improves sleep, too.

Celery for insomnia

Celery has a calming effect on the central nervous system. In fact, celery seed is often used as a herbal remedy for nervousness, insomnia and anxiety. So if you're suffering sleepless nights, take this honey and celery juice mixture:

Add a tablespoonful of honey to a small cup of celery juice, extracted with a juicer.

Sip it slowly half an hour before you go to bed. It should help you relax.

Or if you're not keen on raw celery, try the fantastic recipe for celery soup on page 67 for a sedative supper.

Here are some other tasty ways to get the benefits of celery:

- Add celery (with the leaves on) to soups, stews and casseroles to give them a strong flavour and an extra healthy kick.

- User a juicer to extract the celery juice and mix it with your favourite fruit and vegetables for a healthy punch.

- Sauté the celery in a pan and have it as a side dish. This helps retain most of the potassium in the vegetable, and takes away some of taste you get when you eat it raw.

And finally, if you're still struggling to sleep, try **lavender oil**. Sprinkle a small amount on your pillow before you go to bed. Research suggests it will improve your quality of sleep by 20%.

Basic Celery Soup

Ingredients:
1 whole head of celery chopped (keep the leaves)
A small onion, chopped
A clove of garlic, chopped
250 ml vegetable stock
Salt and ground black pepper

Method:
Shallow fry the onion and celery until soft and translucent, adding the chopped garlic and cooking for another few minutes.

Add the stock and celery leaves, then bring to the boil.

Reduce the heat and simmer for 20 minutes

Season to taste and then liquidise.

CHAPTER 8

Herbs & Spices that Ease Pain

I don't know about you, but I'm loathe to fill my body full of man made drugs to get rid of pain. Why? Because this usually only deadens the symptoms without doing a thing to tackle the root cause of the ailment itself.

But there's a remedy that could change the way we tackle headaches-especially aggressive sinus headaches-for good. Next to migraines, sinus headaches really are the baddest of the bunch. They cause a dull, deep, or severe pain in the front of your head and face that's impossible to ignore.

They are caused by an inflammation to the network of passages that link your forehead, cheeks, nose and eyes. When these passages are working fine, mucus can drain and air can circulate freely, but if the sinuses get inflamed, these areas get blocked and can cause infection.

But, as ever, a little digging around can reveal a whole host of natural remedies that can relieve the misery of sinus headaches.

Barberry *(berberis vulgaris)*, echinacea or eucalyptus all work wonders when it comes to pain relief-plus they can enhance your immune system, prevent colds, and reduce sinus inflammation.

And for a normal, everyday headache, try these great remedies:

- **Feverfew** is a traditional medicinal herb that grows in many gardens (you might even have some hiding in yours), that seems to work by blocking the release of serotonin and prostaglandins, which are thought to be the main culprits behind migraines. By preventing these two substances from doing their work, the blood vessels in your head don't get inflamed. Feverfew has been found to reduce-both the frequency and the severity of migraines – so it's well wortha try. Feverfew supplements usually come in the form of freeze-dried or dried leaves.But you can also get them in capsule, tablet, or liquid extract format. Please consult a professional health provider, or someone qualified in botanical medicine, before trying this remedy. Strong herbs like this should be taken with care. In the case of feverfew there are potential side-effects. Please don't take this remedy if you are pregnant, or on blood-thinning drugs.

- **Head off the start of a headache...** feeling stressed, or having kids leaping up and down at you at the six in the morning, can trigger a headache. So to help manage stress, try the herbs skullcap and wood betony. Both are used to calm the mind and relieve tension, and should be taken throughout the week, particularly if you know it's going to be frantic and you suffer from headaches. They come in tincture form. Again talk to a professional before administering a herbal remedy like this.

- **Jamaican dogwood...** this herb is a different kettle of fish all together. If feverfew is like taking a peashooter to the problem, Jamaican dogwood is like using a cannon. From what I've read, it seems to be very powerful and effective-but it can be toxic in large doses. So whatever you do, DON'T try using this on your own.

- **Boswellia** comes from the boswellia tree. Now there's a surprise! The bit that does you good is the boswellic acid, which acts as an anti-inflammatory to calm down affected areas. This is a great remedy for headaches.

- **Peppermint oil...** an old favourite - just massage into your temples when it feels like there's a Motorhead concert in your head, and the pain should ease.

Another pain-busting tree is known as 'the white willow tree'. It contains a substance called salicin. Again, this converts to a friendly acid in the body (salicylic acid), which tackle the body's pain-producing signals.

A remedy for toothache

For painful toothache or mouth ulcers, you should try salt. Just add salt to room temperature water. Now sloosh it around your mouth, focussing on the infected area. Remember not to swallow. If the problem is really bad, try packing some rock salt crystals around the problem area.

And here's another great little tip for relieving toothache. Dab clove oil onto the effective area to numb the pain. You can get this from your local supermarket or chemist.

Finally, check out vanilla as a remedy. Unfortunately this tip doesn't include vanilla of the ice cream variety. Just dab three or four drops of vanilla extract on a finger and press against the tooth.

How to release your body's natural painkillers

David Perlmutter, M.D, a neurologist in Florida, says that the key to drug-free pain relief is to use your body's natural inflammation-fighting mechanisms. Yes, we all have them. It's just that most people don't know how to switch them on.

To explain it quickly for you, our bodies contain molecules called 'prostaglandins', which come in two distinct types: evil prostaglandins that trigger the inflammation… and good ones that reduce inflammation. So the trick is to take the four natural supplements that switch off evil prostaglandins and turn on the good ones. And here they are:

- **Turmeric.** Yes, we're back to our favourite. As you know this spice contains curcumin, which is a powerful anti-inflammatory. See the first chapter for more details.

- **Bromelain.** This is an enzyme found in pineapples. In a study of injured boxers, the ones taking bromelain healed faster. Ask at your health store for supplements. (Don't take them if you're allergic to pineapple.)

- **Quercitin** is an antihistamine and anti-inflammatory found in onions.

- **Omega-3 and omega-6** essential fatty acids cannot be made by your body, but it needs them to deal with inflammation. Try a tablespoon of flaxseed oil or three capsules of evening primrose oil every day. Or see Chapter 2 for more details.

CHAPTER 9

The Lost Vitamin that Switches on Your Cold & Flu Immunity

Whenever there's a panic about a flu epidemic, the advice for healthy people is always the same. It goes something like this: *Sneeze or cough into your arms if you've no hanky… wash your hands… and if you get the flu, hang on in there and watch* Cash in the Attic *until you feel better or keel over.*

It's a bit like those old 'duck and cover' leaflets from the cold war days: "If there's a nuclear war, hide under your desk." Meanwhile, we're told that clever scientists will take care of all the vulnerable people - the over-70s, children, asthma suffers and pregnant women - with a nice big jab of flu vaccine.

So is that the whole story?

Well, my view on how to protect my family from flu and other nasties was totally transformed by a press release I read on 18th August. It was by Adrian Gombart of Oregon State University. He explained how vitamin D is so important for our survival; it's been conserved in the genome for over 60 million years of evolution.

Gombart says: *"The fact that this vitamin-D mediated immune response has been retained through millions of years of evolutionary selection, and is still found in species ranging from squirrel monkeys to baboons and humans, suggests that it must be critical to their survival."*

He claims that this *"makes it clear that humans and other primates need to maintain sufficient levels of vitamin D."*

The team at Oregon University looked at how vitamin D boosts your immune system by 'turning on' an anti-microbial protein. Gombart writes:

"... This action of 'turning on' an optimal response to microbial attack only works properly in the presence of adequate vitamin D, which is actually a type of hormone that circulates in the blood and signals to cells through a receptor."

Or let me put it in other words. Without enough vitamin D, your immune system doesn't get 'switched on' properly. This leaves you vulnerable to flu - especially in the winter months.

Why flu is worse in winter

It's a well-known fact that flu epidemics get worse in winter. This isn't surprising. Because the main source of vitamin D is *sunlight*.

Back in the 1960s a British researcher called Dr. R. Edgar Hope-Simpson studied influenza. He was the first to spot that something was making humans **less** immune in the winter, and **more** immune in the summer. He predicted that if we could work out why this should be, we could understand, and deal with, serious flu epidemics.

Well, it's now quite clear that this 'something' is vitamin D. Vitamin D doesn't just switch on your immune system... it stops your immune system from over reacting when under attack. It does this by stopping your immune system from releasing too many inflammatory cells, called chemokines and cytokines, into infected lung tissue.

This kind of inflammation was the main cause of death in the 1918 flu pandemic. Usually it manifests itself as bacterial pneumonia. A real killer for the most vulnerable people.

So how can we get enough vitamin D?

Inspired by the Oregon University announcement, my research took me to an article called Epidemic Influenza and Vitamin D by J.J Cannell. This appeared in *Medical News Today* back in September 2006.

Cannell believes that many countries in the West are experiencing a critical vitamin D deficiency In the first instance, there's simply not enough vitamin D in modern human diets. To get enough you'd have to adopt an Innuit-style diet. That is... sardines for breakfast, herring for lunch and salmon for dinner.

However, it's not really food that's the issue. The principal way we get our vitamin D is to absorb it through our skin. And modern humans lose out there, too. Cannell says:

"In the last three hundred years, we began to work indoors; in the last 100 years, we began to travel inside cars; in the last several decades, we began to lather on sunblock and consciously avoid sunlight. All of these things lower vitamin D blood levels. The inescapable conclusion is that vitamin D levels in modern humans are not just low- they are aberrantly low."

So if you can't get adequate amounts of vitamin D from the diet Cannell concludes that *"we must get vitamin D from dietary supplements."*

And here he poses another problem. In his view, the amount of vitamin D in nearly all multivitamins is too inconsequential and has no serious effect on immunity. Most supplements you'll see on sale have 200 to 600iu. This is the usual recommended daily amount. But Cannell says that the best daily dose of vitamin D for adults is 5,000iu per day.

So why not just opt for the flu jab?

Of course, if you're concerned about your vulnerability to swine flu there's always the flu jab. But some reports suggest that this may not be the lifeline it's made out to be. There was an article in *The New York Times* last year that said the following:

"A growing number of immunologists and epidemiologists say the [flu] vaccine probably does not work very well for people over 70, the group that accounts for three-fourths of all flu deaths."

And there's a groundswell of concern about the vaccine's safety, too. Donald W. Miller, MD is a cardiac surgeon and Professor of Surgery at the University of Washington in Seattle. He's also a member of **Doctors for Disaster Preparedness**.

In a very frank article, he says that taking vitamin D is better and safer than a flu shot. He explains what's in many flu jabs…

"Formaldehyde is used to inactivate the virus. It is a known cancer-causing agent. Aluminium is added to promote an antibody response. It is a neurotoxin that may play a role in Alzheimer's disease. Other additives and adjuvants in the flu vaccine… can cause allergic reactions in some people."

And there's more reason to be concerned.

A link to GBS

In August 2009 a letter from the Health Protection Agency was leaked to the *Mail on Sunday*. It told neurologists to be on the lookout for an increase in a brain disorder called Guillain-Barre Syndrome (GBS). It attacks the nerves and can be fatal. They suspect the vaccine could be a trigger for this disease.

A similar swine flu vaccination in the US in the 1970s saw more lives lost because of the jab than through the flu itself. Twenty five people died as a direct result. The US government had to pay out millions in compensation.

So how well has this current flu vaccination been tested? After all, this is being rushed out in the panic, and hasn't gone through the kind of screening process a regular drug would be put through.

I won't add to the scaremongering. But I'd certainly not pin all your hopes on a vaccine. I'd also look into the vitamin D issue.

Make sure you get plenty of sunshine onto your skin whenever you can. And look for high dosage supplements online or ask at your local health food store.

And if you happen to get a simple, old-fashioned cold, please don't fall into the antibiotic trap.

Solve everyday infections without turning to antibiotics

Over the years, the majority of us have gradually been persuaded that natural ways are outdated, and modern remedies brewed up in labs are the answer. And that's causing us a lot of new problems...

According to the Health Protection Agency, 12% of bloodstream infections in the UK caused by E.coli are no longer responding to treatment. Basically, this deadly virus is getting used to the antibiotics we're throwing at it. And because our bodies have become so dependent on these antibiotics, they're in no position to fight back.

It's the equivalent of a rich man suddenly having all his bodyguards deserting him, and being left to face an angry mob on his own. This rich man has been pampered and spoilt and has never thrown a punch in his adult life, so what chance does he have? The truth is, his defences have become lazy, and they've left him open to attack.

Well, the same is happening to people up and down the country. Antibiotics are providing less and less protection-because we've overused them on stupid things like niggly coughs and head colds.

Rather than getting our bodies used to fighting common ailments, we've become reliant on antibiotics to do our fighting for us. Which means that when a serious condition comes along, we need to take stronger antibiotics to fight them, which in turn could cause more side effects.

When NEVER to take antibiotics

As Dr David Livermore, an infections expert at the Health Protection Agency said…

"The NHS must be careful over its use of antibiotics to slow down the development of resistance. GPs should not prescribe, nor patients expect, antibiotics for routine coughs and colds."

I couldn't agree more. Of course, there are going to be times when you need to see your doctor-and there are going to be times when you need to take antibiotics or manmade drugs.

But when it comes to everyday ailments like coughs or colds, I find it incredible that people take drugs when there are powerful, natural remedies that do the job just as well-without the side effects.

I'll give you an example. On the December 2007, a headline in the Daily *Telegraph* proclaimed *"Honey is better at treating children's coughs than an ingredient used in many over-the-counter medicines."*

Researchers had found that children who took honey syrup enjoyed improved sleep, a reduction in coughing frequency and a less bothersome cough. The results were as effective as dextromethorphan, the key ingredient in pricey, mass-produced cough syrups.

And here are some more ways to help your body beat coughs and colds.

- **Ginger** is a powerful, warming herb that fights colds with real gusto. It can help break down the mucus that builds up in your sinuses and lungs, and increases circulation which warms your body. Just grate some fresh ginger into a cup (about one teaspoons should do it), pour on boiling water and let it stand for 10 minutes before sitting down and sipping it.

- **Honey and Lemon.** Take a whole lemon and squeeze the juice into a large mug of hot water. Inhale the steam through your nose for a few minutes, then let it cool a little. Next stir in a teaspoon or two of honey to sweeten it. Then drink.

- **Thyme.** Soak an ounce of dried thyme in a cup of boiled water, cover, until cool. Strain, then mix the liquid with a cup of honey. Now put this into a glass jar and store it in the fridge. Take a teaspoon of this syrup several times a day as needed.

- **Basil.** Take some freshly chopped basil leaves, some crushed raw ginger and add to hot water. Now stir in a teaspoonful of honey and, once cool enough, drink slowly. This will sort out both colds and sore throats.

- **Apples.** An apple a day keeps the sinus headache away. Peel the apple, add a little salt (just a touch) and eat first thing in the morning on an empty stomach. You should find your headache ebbing away.

- **Cinnamon...** but not on your food. Try making a paste of this by mixing it with water, then rub the mixture into your forehead and temples for relief. Messy, but at least you can ditch the pill bottle.

CHAPTER 10

The Purple Salad that Boosts Stamina & Lowers Your Blood Pressure

Where would we be without the rich and famous? They're not content with singing, dancing, battling aliens, eating maggots in the jungle, falling out of taxis, jumping on Oprah's sofa, buying African children, bankrolling The Priory and marrying each other… divorcing each other… and marrying each other again. They are now HEALTH PIONEERS!

First came the celebrity fitness videos…

As you know, exercise ***didn't*** exist until Jane Fonda got involved. We used to lie all day on brown 70s sofas, eating lard, until good old Jane came along.

Then came the celebrity diets…

South Beach, Atkins, Blood Type, Raw Food. You name it, yet another A-list celebrity's weight was yo-yoing higher and lower than… well… a yo-yo.

Then came the celebrity injections…

First, botox. Suddenly celebs were walking around with faces like wax models of dinner plates. Actresses couldn't act any more. They now looked like plastic *Billy Bass* novelty singing fish.

Then came the latest: vitamin B12 jabs.

The Madonna effect

In 2008, Madonna was merrily brandishing a syringe, gushing about the B12 effect. And, allegedly, Tara Palmer-Tomkinson, Geri Halliwell and Robbie Williams all swear by the stuff.

The idea is that you get a big shot of B12 directly into your body. It's about 600 times more than the daily recommended amount of 1.5mcg. This gives you an energy rush that lasts about a fortnight. It's supposed to be good for skin and general well-being, too.

So is this worth checking out? Well, first off, do not attempt to give yourself a shot of vitamin B12 and don't 'phone a friend' either. If you're going to get this treatment, you MUST go through a medical professional. If you go through the proper channels, then there's no likely danger in the short term.

A review of a B12 conducted by the Food Standards Agency a few years ago was inconclusive about injections of high doses of B12 into the bloodstream. The only reservation it had was regarding the long-term effects. However, Catherine Collins, the chief dietician at St George's Hospital in London warned in an interview with the *Daily Mail*:

"The digestive system ordinarily acts as a filter with food and to some extent oral supplements, making it actually quite difficult to overdose on nutrients. But by bypassing the gut and going straight into veins, the body is unable to perform its natural screening process."

Do you really need this injection?

It seems that there are a fair few types of people who SHOULD enquire with their doctor about B12.

- **Elderly people with symptoms including tremors, tiredness and other neurological symptoms.** It's estimated that 10% 15% of people over the age of 60 have a vitamin B12 deficiency. This can lead to all the above problems.

- **People with pernicious anaemia.** Normal anaemia is caused by lack of iron. But pernicious anaemia occurs when your body kills off the B12 you eat. This means that eating more foods containing vitamin B12 won't cure the problem.

- **Some vegetarians and vegans.** Because B12 is found mainly in meat, fish and dairy products, some vegetarians who experience a deficiency may need the shots for a quicker recovery. Saying that, long-term vegans and vegetarians are said to be more efficient at absorbing B12 from foods. You can also get B12 from Brewer's yeast. But not all nutritional yeast products contain B12. So make sure you read the label.

- **Heavy drinkers and smokers, pregnant and breast-feeding women.** Sometimes they can also need an extra boost of vitamin B12. Although they CAN get this vitamin from their food.

However, most people need only a B12 supplement, or to up their intake of B12 foods, which include mussels, oysters, clams, liver, beef, lamb, trout, salmon, eggs and hard cheeses. Using the shot simply as an energy booster doesn't look much more than a fad of the jet-set crowd. It's particularly good for hangovers apparently, so it fits the pop-star lifestyle.

It makes it the latest 'in-thing' for rich, bored celebrities who spend half their lives drunk, and the other half in therapy moaning about drink.

If you want to give yourself a homemade shot of energy, then try this less painful option instead.

The purple vegetable that boosts stamina

This year a research team, led by the University of Exeter, has discovered that drinking a glass of beetroot juice can boost your stamina. The nitrate in beetroot juice causes a reduction in your uptake of oxygen. This slows the rate at which you become tired. The study claims that if you're doing strenuous exercise, you'll be able to keep going for 16% longer.

And there's only one side effect. This is one that I noticed only the other week when I went to the loo in the morning. I nearly fainted when I saw the red colour in the toilet bowl. My old hypochondria came flooding back.

"My god I am going to die!" muttered my paranoid brain.

Thankfully, my endless days and nights musing over food and health issues came to the rescue. *I suddenly knew what the problem was.* Eating a lot of beetroot or drinking beetroot juice can lead to something called beeturia, which turns your urine a very scary red. I'd completely forgotten that I'd eaten a beetroot salad the night before!

But hey, as side effects go, there are plenty worse. And beetroot is a food worth getting into your system for other reasons. Research by Barts and the London School of Medicine and the Peninsula Medical School, in 2008 found that beetroot juice reduced your blood pressure.

And it's good for your heart, too. Beetroot contains a powerful little substance called betaine, which can help lower your levels of homocysteine. This has been linked with heart disease if it's produced too keenly. So getting betaine into your system helps make sure homocysteine doesn't build up.

Tasty ways to get beetroot into your diet

To get your beetroot fix, boil some beetroot 'til soft, or get hold of pre-cooked beetroot in its own juices (not vinegar). You can then juice yourself some of the pure stuff.

Or take a couple of apples, a couple of carrots, and some cooked beetroot. Now juice them together. This is far more palatable in my opinion.

My other tip is to try this salad. Take some fresh salad leaves, chopped spring onion, a handful of crushed walnuts, some crumbled feta cheese, thinly sliced celery and slices or chunks of beetroot. Make a dressing out of lemon, oil, parsley, salt and pepper.

Delicious Antioxidant Salad

Ingredients:
Lettuce leaves
4 tbsp chopped Brazil nuts
4 tbsp chopped dates
2 tomatoes, sliced
2 carrots, grated
2 raw beetroots, grated
About 12 oz grated cabbage
1/2 cucumber, sliced
Vinaigrette of your choice

Method:
Place lettuce leaves on plates. Combine the Brazil nuts and the chopped dates and put them in a pile in the middle of the plate. Add the other vegetables in piles around the nuts and create an appetizing and colourful dish.

Just before serving, pour a bit of vinaigrette over the salad to moisten.

This is perfect as a super-healthy vegetarian appetizer or even as a light lunch eaten with some crusty bread.

Recipe courtesy of Natural Mom's Recipes,
www.naturalmomsrecipes.com

Ray's Beetroot and Feta Salad

Salad ingredients:
4 small cooked beetroots
Half a block of feta cheese
Rocket
4 spring onions, finely chopped
Handful of chopped Walnuts
10 cherry tomatoes, halved

For the dressing:
1 tbsp apple cider vinegar
3 tbsp virgin olive oil
Salt and pepper
Finely chopped parsley

Method:
Mix the rocket, onions, chopped walnuts and cherry tomatoes in a bowl. Add the dressing.

Place the salad on the plate. Now add slices of beetroot and crumble over with feta cheese, or add cubes of diced feta cheese if you prefer. Sprinkle the chopped onion on top and serve with bread.

Pick-me-up Morning Juice

Ingredients:
11 large green apples, cored and coarsely chopped
1 large beetroot, peeled and coarsely chopped
2 inch piece of fresh ginger, coarsely chopped

Method:
If you own a juice extractor, push all ingredients through extractor.

If not, process ingredients in a food processor until smooth. Use a sieve with a fine mesh and push through. Enjoy this healthy addition to breakfast!

Recipe courtesy of Natural Mom's Recipes,
www.naturalmomsrecipes.com

CHAPTER 11

The Muffin that Fights Cancer

"The muffin that fights cancer?" you gasp. Could there be such a bizarre and miraculous thing? Next I'll be saying, "The Twix that Cures Heart Disease", "The Lager that Makes You Ten Years Younger", "The Cigar that Cures Asthma' or 'The Poke in the Eye With A Big Stick that Reverses Blindness".

But don't just take my humble word for it. This was published in the *American Institute for Cancer Research Newsletter* back in 1998. The journal refers to a remarkable little study with huge potential. Researchers at the University of Toronto took 39 women with breast cancer. They gave half of them a plain muffin to eat for 5 and-a-half weeks. The other half also ate a muffin. But this contained 25 gm of flaxseed oil.

Researchers found a **33% reduction** in the growth of the tumours in those who ate the flaxseed muffins.

"Our results are very exciting because this is the first time anyone has demonstrated these changes in breast cancer with any dietary component." says Dr. Paul Goss, director of the breast cancer prevention program at the Toronto Hospital.

There are two theories for this phenomenon. One is that the fibre in the flax seed gets rid of the excess oestrogen. Other research has shown that increasing the amount of fibre in your diet reduces your risk of other cancers too… including cancer of the colon.

The second theory is that flax blocks your oestrogen receptors. By doing so, it lowers the rate of tumour growth. So flax is something that could significantly help women AND men with cancer.

But it has a powerful role to play in *prevention* too…

Flax is very high in compounds called 'lignans'. Many researchers believe these compounds can help protect us against cancer. Flax seed is also high in alpha linolenic acid (ALA). This is a form of plant-based **omega 3 fatty acid.** Many believe this is another promising cancer fighting agent.

And the benefits don't stop there…

How to ease the symptoms of Crohn's disease, depression and the menopause

Other possible benefits of flax include lowering of bad cholesterol levels, lowering of triglyceride levels, and reducing your blood pressure.

Recent studies suggest that flax seed oil can ease the symptoms of Crohn's disease and colitis. These are ailments that affect your digestive system. Many naturopaths recommend that taking flax seed oil can help calm and soothe your inflamed intestines.

And finally, by taking a regular moderate amount of flax seed oil, you could even improve your mood.

Research by Dr. Martha Clare Morris of Chicago's St. Luke's Medical Center claims that a diet rich in omega-3 fatty acids could ease depression and help maintain your brain function. And flax seed is absolutely packed with these fatty acids.

To make a healthy bread enriched with flaxseed, try the recipe on page 95. Or for a quicker fix, try the delicious 'power breakfast smoothie'.

Before I leave you to try those recipes, here's another remarkable food that many believe could fight cancer. It's something many of my newsletter readers write to me about, usually with gushing praise.

Could an apricot help fight cancer?

The ancient Egyptians were the first to discover how to extract a powerful poison from peach or apricot kernels. There's a papyrus in the Louvre which shows the earliest recording of preparing cyanide.

The text warns: 'Pronounce not the name of I.A.O [God] under the penalty of the peach.'

Under penalty of the *peach*. How strange… but probably an effective deterrent when Egyptians found out that cyanide extracted from peach kernels could kill people stone dead (excuse the pun!)

However, modern science didn't discover the chemistry behind this until 1802. In that year, a chemist called Bohn discovered that when he distilled the water from bitter almonds, hydrocyanic acid was released. This was hydrogen cyanide. The stuff that threatened the lives of blasphemous Egyptians.

A few years later, a couple of scientists managed to isolate a white substance in hydrogen cyanide. It's known as Vitamin B17 or, more commonly, 'amygdalin'.

Amygdalin is what's known as a 'cyanide radical'. In simple terms, this means that it has some of the properties of cyanide, but can also change the nature of cells. While hydrogen cyanide is the lethal stuff that killed Nazi ogres like Herman Goering, amygdalin is a totally different kind of substance. Scientists have shown that, in small doses, amygdalin is safe.

For instance, this is a substance that you can find in fruits packed with vitamin B12. You consume it whenever you eat blackberries, blueberries and strawberries.

So what has this cyanide radical known as vitamin B17 got to do with cancer? Cyanide radicals may not harm you in natural amounts, but they do some terrible things to cancerous cells. Normal, healthy cells in our bodies contain an enzyme called rhodanese. This enzyme neutralises the amygdalin (vitamin B17) and stops it from releasing hydrogen cyanide.

But for cancer cells, it's another matter. They DON'T contain the enzyme Rhodanese. Without it, the amygdalin releases cyanide and begins destroying these malignant cells.

Here you have something that potentially kills the bad cancer cells and spares the good. This stuff is like Clint Eastwood on a mission. But the mainstream medical attitude towards B17 has not been at all positive.

Eighteen years ago, some of the world's top scientists claimed that vitamin B17 could help in the prevention of cancer - and perhaps even KILL existing cancer cells.

Great news, surely? Well no. Because this was just an extract of apricot stones, it couldn't be patented by pharmaceutical companies to make tonnes of cash. So the drug barons demanded that more studies be conducted. They stirred up fear, controversy and suspicion.

In the US, the Food and Drug Administration has banned the interstate shipment and sale of Vitamin B17. They alleged that it's either an 'unlicensed new 'drug' or an 'unsafe or adulterated food or food additive'.

Of course, as you now know, it comes from apricot kernels. But that hasn't stopped information about vitamin B17 being brushed under the carpet. I mean, even if the scientists are wrong, don't you have the right to know that you could protect yourself with this vitamin?

How to find and take Vitamin B17

First you need to consult a medical professional if you are worried about cancer or any serious illness. Always talk to a doctor about big dietary changes.

If you wish to get mild doses of B17 through your everyday diet, you can find the highest amounts of vitamin B17 in bitter almonds, apple, apricot, cherry, nectarine, peach, pear, plum and prune. It's also in beans, chickpeas, cashew nuts, blackberries, cranberries, elderberries, raspberries and strawberries.

You should eat the above fruits whole. If you wish to try the kernels, many naturopaths recommend 6-10 apricot kernels per day. However official health bodies recommend a consumption of no more than 2

Kernels per day. In any case, the kernels should not be swallowed whole. They need to be ground and sprinkled on food or in fruit juice.

Get your seeds at your local health store or type 'buy apricot kernels UK' into a search engine like www.google.com and see what comes up.

Flax Seed Bread

Ingredients:
50g whole wheat flour
2 tsp brown sugar, honey or dark treacle
200g bread flour
1 tsp salt
50g flax seeds or flax meal
Handful of sunflower seeds
175ml water
1 tsp instant yeast

Method:
NOTE: If you have whole flax seeds, leave half whole and put half in a coffee grinder. Flax absorbs a lot of water, which could make the bread a little heavy for your taste, so try and soak them overnight, then add to the mix so they don't suck up all the water for the dough.

Take a large bowl and mix together the dry flour, salt, flax seed, malt, sunflower seeds and yeast.

Stir in water and mix again. Shape the mix into a ball. It should be very sticky. Now knead the dough.

Place the mix in a bowl greased with butter. Cover it and leave at room temperature to rise for an hour and a half.

Now shape into a loaf, put on a greased baking tray. Cover and give it another 60 minutes.

Now lightly brush with water and put in oven a 200 °C for 45 minutes.

Power Breakfast Smoothie

Ingredients:
1 banana, chopped
1 kiwi, peeled
1/2 apple, chopped
125g of frozen mixed berries
250ml orange juice
125ml milk
125g plain yogurt
3 tbsp unsalted peanut butter
2 tbsp flax seed oil

Method:
Combine the various fruits and orange juice in a blender and process everything until nice and smooth. Add the rest of the ingredients and blend until well mixed.

Enjoy this very healthy breakfast smoothie that is rich in antioxidants, vitamins, and fibre and that will give you the best possible start to your day.

Recipe courtesy of Natural Mom's Recipes,
www.naturalmomsrecipes.com

CHAPTER 12

The Cabbage that Cures Impotence & Fatigue

I've never been so out of breath as when I visited Machu Picchu. This ancient Incan ruin is hidden high up in the Peruvian Andes, more than 2,500 metres above sea level. At that height, the air is so thin your lungs gasp and your head spins with the altitude.

Despite me wheezing like it was my last day on earth, it was probably one of the most memorable places I visited when I went to South America in my 20's. At the time, I decided it was a good idea to shove loads of coca leaves into my mouth for an energy boost.

Well, the guides were doing it, and I was game for anything.

The idea is that you chew on a wedge of leaves over the course of the day. It releases small doses of energy into your bloodstream, and makes you resistant to the altitude. The locals who live at these high altitudes depend on it to keep working.

Coca is South America's most famous and controversial crop. It's revered there for its restorative powers, but hated by governments who dislike what it can be turned into - namely, cocaine.

However, there's another crop from Peru that gets far less international attention. But its powers as a source of energy are now well known in natural health circles. Here's a list of just some of its reported benefits...

• Boosts libido, stamina and endurance

• Helps decrease erectile dysfunction and impotency

• Increases energy

• Improves mood and mental agility

• Reduces menopausal symptoms

• Regulates menstruation and period pains

• Improves testosterone levels

You'll be amazed to know that the plant that can do this looks a bit like a potato, is shaped like a giant radish, and is related to the cabbage family.

The cabbage that could solve an embarrassing problem

The plant is called maca, or 'lepidium meyenii'. It is the only plant that can survive at up to 4,000 metres above sea level in South America. Doing so, it has to cope with severe heat during the day… and then freezing cold at night. Believe me, I camped up there during my Machu Picchu trek in five layers of clothing, under two blankets, and in a sleeping bag tighter than a sock. And STILL I was cold.

But the benefits of it achieving this endurance feat are immense. The soil in which maca grows is packed full of minerals. This makes maca unusually high in vitamins, essential amino acids and important fatty acids.

The locals in some of these remote Andean communities have eaten the stuff for years, of course. But elsewhere the knowledge of it died out. It was only after the 60s when German and North American scientists went into these remote villages to study the plant life, that maca was re-introduced to the world.

Since then, maca has garnered a stronger reputation as the 'Peruvian Viagra'. And, yes, one if its main uses is as a solution to various problems in the bedroom.

It can help fight erectile dysfunction and impotency. It can increase libido and desire in both men and women. And it offers a decent energy boost too. But it's actually quite different to Viagra. For one thing, it can help both men AND women in the bedroom. And for another, users claim it has significant benefits for a variety of hormonal problems.

A natural hormone regulator

For men, maca also increases the testosterone level, and improves energy level, sporting performance and stamina.

Women use maca to ease the symptoms of peri-menopause, menopause and post-menopause. And many women even use it as a safe and natural alternative for hormone replacement therapy (HRT). In one report I read, Dr Gabriel Cousens says he prefers maca to conventional hormone replacement therapy (HTP, DHEA, pregnenolone, or fitoe-strogenes).

"Maca is a balanced answer to the effects of an aging endocrine system. HRT declines the capacity of the endocrine glands to produce hormones; this fosters the aging of the body."

For more information on alternatives to HRT, please see the next chapter.

Another great benefit of taking Maca

Finally, maca is packed with calcium, containing 350mgs-500mgs per 100 grams. This makes it a more powerful alternative to milk, without the dairy. And it also makes it a good supplement to take if you want to increase your bone density. This makes it well worth considering if you suffer from osteoporosis.

Maca is really easy to take. It's available in a supplement form, either as a tablet or a powder. Make sure you follow the correct dosage as stated on the label. If you decide to try it out please heed this word of warning. There are a lot of companies peddling sub-standard Maca on the internet. Some of it is grown in Europe, which means it doesn't contain the same level of nutrients as the real stuff from South America.

If you want to try Maca that's genuinely from Peru, try out this website: www.maca.co.uk/goodlifeletter. These guys offer a really good service and product. Or you can ask about it at your local health store.

Maca is only a distant Latin American cousin to the cabbage we know and love. But our humble British cabbage, both the red and green versions, is also a fantastically healthy food.

How a cabbage could protect you from ulcers and dementia

I'll admit, I hated cabbage as a kid. The word 'cabbage' conjured up images of an earth-smeared, green monster with a frilly face, bad breath and the taste of a witch's underpants. Thinking about it now, perhaps I had a slightly disturbed imagination,

But say "cabbage" to any adult and you'll still get a few people screwing their faces up in disgust. Few realise that a cabbage can help you burn fat, protect your skin, relieve ulcer problems, cleanse your liver and colon, and even protect your brain cells.

As you can imagine cabbage is a pretty good weight loss food. It's a green leafy vegetable after all, one of the best kinds of whole food you can eat. And a cup's worth of it contains only 15 calories.

Better still, it contains:

- **Phytonutrients,** these help protect you from free radicals (cancer causing agents) that can damage your cell walls.

- **Lactic acid,** this can help disinfect your colon.

- **Sulforaphane,** a substance that stimulates the production of glutathione. This is an antioxidant which can help clean your liver of impurities.

- **Vitamin E,** an anti-oxidant that helps your skin look glowing and healthy. You can even keep wrinkles at bay. Just mix 30 ml of cabbage juice with a teaspoon of honey. Dab this on your face every evening and leave for 20 minutes.

- **Vitamin C** many believe that this helps your cells to burn fat.

- **Vitamin A,** this is important for your eye health.

Also, if you eat red cabbage you get a dose of ***anthocyanin***, which is responsible for its red colour. This antioxidant helps protect your brain cells. Many scientists now believe it could have a role in the fight against Alzheimer's.

Anthocyanins also have potential as 'fat-fighters'. So claims a Japanese study carried out in February 2008. According to the *Journal of Agricultural and Food Chemistry*, these antioxidants in red cabbage could help tackle metabolic syndrome (MetS). This can cause obesity, hyper-tension, insulin problems.

The quickest way to get the benefits of cabbage is to drink 25-50 ml of fresh, raw cabbage juice each day. During the early 1950s, Dr Garnett Cheney found that peptic ulcer patients who drank 4 glasses of raw cabbage juice daily quickened the healing process and relieved the pain.

A juicer and a cabbage is all you need. It's pretty simple.

However, I like to find ways that you can enjoy really genuinely tasty meals and still get all the benefits of something like cabbage. After all, good health is about enjoyment and adventure, not just chucking down medicine. So try the cabbage salad recipe overleaf. This was one sent in by a Good Life Letter reader and works really well.

Another Latin American marvel

To finish, I'd like to take you all the way back to Latin America. This time Central America, where another type of cabbage has long been regarded as a medicine. The Coallis Lombarda cabbage contains high doses of a powerful vitamin called Vitamin U. This is one of nature's strongest weapons against gastric and intestinal disorders.

Dr. GarnettCheney, professor of medicine at Stanford Medical School, published a report about the use of Vitamin U in the treatment of gastric ulcer. Of 65 cases reported, 62 were cured at the end of three weeks.

No wonder this small, red cabbage has been a natural medicine since times of the Mayan civilization.

It's hard to find this cabbage in the UK so you'll be lucky to get your hands on one. But ordinary raw cabbage also contains smaller amounts of vitamin U. Try the recipe overleaf and see how it works for you.

Cabbage Salad

Ingredients
Half a head of cabbage) - very finely shredded
1 1/2 cups celery leaves - finely chopped
1/2 large onion or one small onion (+-80g) - very finely chopped

Dressing
50ml good quality vinegar
200ml sunflower oil (you can use olive oil but it does change the taste a little)
1 tbsp fine white sugar
1/2 tbsp fine white salt (more or less to taste if desired)
1 tsp fine white pepper or black pepper
1/2 tsp mustard powder

Method:
Place the cabbage, celery leaves and onion into large bowl.
Next combine all the dressing ingredients in a 500ml bottle with a tightly fitting lid. Vigorously shake the bottle until mixture is completely blended and has the consistency of warm honey.

Pour this over the cabbage salad. Toss and allow the mixture to stand for at least 10 minutes in the fridge.

Now serve and eat!

CHAPTER 13

The Stew that Helps You Though the Menopause

Robert A Wilson, a New York gynaecologist, had a real way with words. The granddaddy of Hormone Replacement Therapy (HRT), he was the first to call the menopause a "deficiency disease". Now there's a man who knows how to make an older woman feel good.

But the dear doctor didn't stop there.

The doctor with bedside manner deficiency disease

In words that wouldn't get him very far in the chat-up stakes, he described post-menopausal women as "shrivelled into caricatures of their former selves" and "castrates".

Castrates? Was he slightly barmy or did he just not really know what that meant? If not, my wife could recommend plenty of women out there who'd love to have given him a first-hand demonstration.

Now, if you're feeling generous, you could put Robert's words down to him being 'of his time' and a little daft. But I reckon he knew exactly what he was doing. By making menopausal women feel like wizened old has-beens, he then positioned himself as their saviour, with a magic bullet that would solve all their problems.

It's a dirty little trick, and it goes something like this...

The dirtiest marketing trick in the book.

You go up to the make-up counter to buy mascara, only to walk away with a shed-load of expensive creams after the beautician's told you they're the only thing that can save your sorry-looking skin before it shrivels up and falls off. Or something like that.

Well, Dr Wilson's spiel was even dodgier, because back in the 1960s, his magic bullet was oestrogen replacement therapy. With a $1.3 million subsidy from – you guessed it – the pharmaceutical companies, Robbie-dear set up a private trust dedicated to promoting oestrogen drugs-the first real HRT.

It was all going so well. Until scientists finally clocked that the treatment led to an increase in breast and ovarian cancer, not to mention fibroids and gall bladder disease.

Of course, HRT has come on leaps and bounds since then and today's drugs are a far cry from the ones Wilson was promoting. But like an annoying fly, the link to breast cancer refuses to go away. There have been several studies of HRT which have made the link. But this was the most famous.

The cancer discovery that shocked the world

The Million Women Study was published in *The Lancet* in 2003. The results were so shocking, it made front page headlines at the time. Having followed a million women, the study found that those who'd used HRT had double the risk of breast cancer.

In June 2004, a symposium on hormones, women and cancer risk, at Radcliffe Institute for Advanced Studies, accused pharmaceutical companies of colluding to make the menopause a deficiency disease: one that needed *pills* rather than natural preventative solutions.

A report asked: *"Why, for four decades, since the mid 1960s, were millions of women prescribed powerful pharmacological agents already shown, three decades earlier, to be carcinogenic?"*

You'd think that would spell the end for HRT. But no. In spite of everything, HRT remains a multi-million pound industry with a big marketing budget and some serious weight behind it. Until recently the mainstream media was trumpeting HRT drug Prempro as a 'one pill wonder'. Just swallow it down and say goodbye to hot flushes, heart disease, everything!

A few years ago Prempro was linked to an increased risk of breast cancer and Alzheimer's. Since then it seems that we're being bombarded with negative stories about HRT every month. And don't get me wrong-HRT does minimise menopausal symptoms like hot flushes.

But for many women, the benefits come at way too high a price. If you want to read more about the research and studies behind HRT, I recommend the book ***Food Is Better Medicine Than Drugs*** by Patrick Holford and Jerome Burns.

This fascinating read lays bare the reality behind many of the magic bullet treatments around today-from HRT to statins. It might not sound it from the title, but this book does give you a balanced view so you've the space to make up your own mind.

It also suggests some well-researched natural alternatives to HRT. So if you're someone who's decided against taking HRT, this will interest you.

Natural ways to alleviate the symptoms of the menopause

- **Tuck into some tofu, beans or chickpeas.** They're all packed with isoflavones, a plant substance that's similar to oestrogen. Studies have shown that the higher the isoflavone levels you have, the less likely you are to have hot flushes. And unlike HRT they've been shown to protect against cancer. See the recipe at the end of this chapter for a stew that will lift your isoflavone levels.

- **Sage** is another tasty option. According to a 2005 study at the Queensland University of Technology, Brisbane, sage reduces severe hot flushes by 60% compared with a placebo. To make sage tea take 10 fresh leaves, or one and a half teaspoons of the dried stuff (fresh is better). Pour over the leaves and add a spoon or two of honey to sweeten it. Drink this about an hour before you go to bed.

- **Black cohosh** is another popular herb for anxiety, hot flushes and night sweats. In terms of rigorous medical testing, the jury is still out, but there's plenty of anecdotal testimony.

- **Flaxseed.** For some people flax can reduce hot flushes and other menopausal symptoms. This is because flax is a phytoestrogen, an oestrogen-like substance found in plants. This means flax can be used as a natural hormone stabiliser.

- **Maca.** This is a Peruvian vegetable, related to the cabbage. It's another well-regarded hormone regulator. For more details see the previous chapter.

- **Dan shen** a herb widely used in Traditional Chinese Medicine (TCM) for improving blood circulation, regulating menstruation and relieving insomnia.

- **Wild yam** (Rhizome discorea) is a common herbal remedy for menopause symptoms.

- **Dong quai** is another herb, good for the menopause. In one study from 2003, 55 postmenopausal women who were given dong quai and chamomile instead of HRT had an 80% reduction in hot flushes after a month. It doesn't seem to have any cancer-promoting properties either. It does thin the blood though, so avoid it if you're taking warfarin.

- **Jiaogulan,** a Chinese herb that reduces stress, and regulates blood pressure and cholesterol.

- **Kiwi fruit extract,** which helps with digestion and absorbing all the above ingredients.

- **You can also use bioflavanoids and vitamin C and vitamin E to reduce the severity of hot flushes.** Try seeking out supplements, or adding plenty of fresh fruit and raw vegetables to your daily diet.

If you're worried about HRT's links to breast cancer, many experts suggest that you can use preventatives like folic acid and thiamine. Please consult a medical expert for the correct doses and check with your doctor first.

Spicy Four Bean Chilli Stew

Ingredients:

1 can organic chilli beans (seasoned dark red), do not drain
2 cans organic spicy pinto beans, do not drain
1 can organic chick peas, do not drain
6 pieces dried tofu, 1 package, soaked in warm water 5 minutes
1 can organic chopped tomatoes, do not drain
1 can organic diced tomatoes with green chillies (try Eden Organics), do not drain
2 tbsp extra virgin olive oil
2 cloves garlic, minced
1 medium onion, diced
100g celery, diced
150g carrots, diced
200g organic sweet corn, fresh or frozen
2 tsp soy sauce, or to taste

Directions:

Heat the oil in a large pot and sauté the garlic and onions for 1 to 2 minutes.

Add the celery and carrots, and sauté another 1 to 2 minutes.

Add all of the beans and tomatoes along with their cooking liquid.

Squeeze the water out of the soaked dried tofu and discard the water. Grate the tofu on a cheese grater. If some of the pieces are large, simply break them into smaller pieces with your fingers.

Place the grated dried tofu in the soup pot. Cover and bring to a boil. Reduce the flame and simmer for 20 to 25 minutes.

Add the soy sauce, cover and simmer another 5 minutes. Serve hot.

Recipe courtesy of Eden Foods,
www.edenfoods.com

Scrambled Tofu with Turmeric

Ingredients:
1 tbsp extra virgin olive oil
100g onion, diced
100g button mushrooms, stems removed, sliced
200g organic sweet corn, fresh or frozen
200g carrots, julienned
500g organic extra firm tofu, rinsed and drained
2 tsp soy sauce or plum vinegar
100g spring onions, finely sliced
1/4 tsp freshly ground black pepper
1 tsp turmeric

Method:
Heat the oil in a large skillet and sauté the onions and mushrooms for 2 to 3 minutes. Add the carrots and sweet corn. With your hands crumble the tofu on top of the vegetables. Sprinkle the soy sauce or plum vinegar over the tofu, cover and reduce the flame to medium-low. Cook for 5 minutes or until the tofu fluffs up like scrambled eggs. Remove the cover, turn the flame to high, mix in the spring onions, black pepper and turmeric. Cook another 2 to 3 minutes, stirring frequently until all liquid from the tofu evaporates. Serve hot for breakfast, lunch or dinner.

Note: Sliced Shiitake Mushrooms can be substituted for button mushrooms. Simply soak the mushrooms in warm water to cover for 10 minutes, remove, drain and follow above directions. The shiitake soaking water can be saved and used for making soup stock, if desired.

Recipe courtesy of Eden Foods,
www.edenfoods.com

CHAPTER 14

The Garden Weed that Cleans Your Liver

I'm not much of a gardener. Once, when I was younger, I planted a pot with herb seeds and stuck it in my tiny, ramshackle garden. After a few weeks I was pleased to see my herbs flourishing. I kept watering the pot and watching this lovely green foliage rise from the soil.

I even showed it to one of my friends when she came round for a barbeque one afternoon.

"What do you think?" I said, proudly.

"Ray, that's a weed," she said.

Yes indeed. I'd been lovingly growing a garden weed in a pot. Percy

Thrower, eat your heart out. Perhaps if I'd bothered to try the herb in a salad, instead of feasting on takeaways, I would have realised my mistake sooner.

Things have changed a bit since then. I can not only tell the difference between weeds and herbs, my entire outlook on weeds has changed. Because it turns out that some weeds are very powerful natural medicines.

One in particular is *extremely* common. You'll find it right now in any park or garden that hasn't been too looked after. Use it in the right way, and it could help you soothe muscle and joint aches, ease urinary problems, dissolve gallstones, improve your digestion, control your blood pressure and regulate your heart. Best of all, this medicine is absolutely free.

Which makes it a recession-proof alternative to expensive, chemical-laden drugs that line that pockets of mega-wealthy multinationals.

The amazing benefits of the common dandelion

For centuries, dandelions have been an important folk medicine in the northern hemisphere. They are known to be a diuretic, which means they control and regulate your trips to the loo. If you suffer from water retention, urinary problems or bad digestion, you'll find dandelions a gentle way to ease your problems. Most diuretics flush important minerals like potassium from your body.

But not dandelion. *It's packed with the stuff.*

Potassium helps regulate your blood pressure and keep your heart functioning properly. It's important for people with hypertension. In one Harvard study, men who took potassium with a diuretic (which is essentially what dandelion is) *decreased their stroke risk by 60%.*

Dandelion also contains many other vital antioxidants, vitamins and minerals. Which is why it's such a popular alternative medicine for those 'in-the-know'.

According to Linda Gray author of **Grow Your Own Pharmacy:**
"Over the centuries poultices and potions have been made from dandelions to treat many conditions, including colds, ulcers, and obesity. The dandelion is said to be helpful in dissolving gallstones and even alleviating pain due to heart conditions."

And Joy Mary, an e-magazine writer from the USA says:

"[Dandelion] is a wonderful liver cleaner and increases the output of the liver, the flow of bile into the intestines and the activity of the pancreas and spleen. This makes it a great treatment for hepatitis, yellow jaundice, and other liver-related problems."

There are loads of ways I've found to prepare and use dandelion. You can dab the sap from the stem on to warts and verrucas a few times every day. Or turn the flowers from the dandelion into a jam.

You can use the young leaves as a healthy extra ingredient in a summer salad. They're quite bitter, so add plenty of tomatoes, honey dressing and other goodies to balance it out. For hot meals you can sauté the leaves with vegetables like onions, garlic and carrots. Or you can make a dandelion tea. To make this, simply infuse the leaves in hot water.

For **a super-healing tea,** try a tablespoon of dandelion leaves, a table-spoon of nettle leaves and about a third of a litre of boiling water. Steep for 10 minutes then strain.

Apparently, drinking four cups of dandelion tea each day is good for fibromyalgia sufferers... especially if you add burdock root and red clover. This potent combination helps boost your body's immune system and cleans out your bloodstream.

If you're pregnant, please don't try these dandelion tips until you've spoken to your doctor. And if you're worried about a serious medical condition, also speak to a health professional. Finally, if you're collecting dandelions from parks or fields, make sure that they haven't been blitzed with pesticides and herbicides. To make doubly sure, always wash wild flowers and plants thoroughly before use.

Some more medicines you may have at home

There's a whole range of 'natural medicines' you can start growing in your garden:

- **Tomatoes...** tomatoes are loaded with lycopene, a carotenoid which has been linked with prevention of certain cancers, such as prostate cancers.

And that's just the start of the mighty tomato's protective powers... a study in Israel showed that a good dose of tomato can help lower blood pressure and reduce the risk of heart disease. This study looked at patients who were being treated for hypertension, but weren't reacting well with the drugs. Instead, they were given doses of tomato extract.

The result? A significant lowering of blood pressure after just four weeks.

- **Beetroots...** beetroot contains a powerful little substance called betaine, which acts like a really old-fashioned cleaning lady and sweeps out homocysteine with ruthless efficiency. Beetroot juice is also said to 'awaken' your body's natural antioxidant functions.

See chapter 10 for more details.

- **Carrot...** Carrots have a ton of goodies in them: calcium, iron, essential carbs, proteins, vitamins B1, B2, B6, C and K, niacin, potassium. Carrots can help your body fight fatigue, diabetes, stroke, eye problems and inflammation.

Three essential kitchen cupboard ingredients you can rely on

- **Honey...** honey is good for us in so many ways. It's packed with antioxidants, the powerful little compounds which fight free radicals. In a 2004 study at the University of California, 25 people were asked to eat between four and 10 tablespoons of buckwheat honey each day for a month. They could eat the honey in almost any form, but it couldn't be baked or dissolved in tea. After the month was up, the researchers analysed the blood of all 25 people, and discovered that eating more honey had increased the level of polyphenolic antioxidants in the blood.

- **Garlic...** this brilliant little ingredient has been linked to dozens of great health benefits, including lowering cholesterol and blood pressure, and cutting down the threat of stroke and heart disease. In one study, a group of people who added garlic to their diets over a month enjoyed a 12% drop in cholesterol levels. And the *Journal of Hypertension* reported that taking garlic tablets could cut the risk of stroke by 30%-40%, and the risk of heart disease by 20%-25%.

- **Vinegar...** vinegar is packed with healthy nutrients, including potassium-a mineral that helps relieve cramps, fatigue and heart arhythmia.

9 more surprising natural health remedies

- **Fennel tea for flatulence!** Little known fact: fennel can treat mild stomach problems like feeling over-full or flatulence. To make your own fennel tea, add half a teaspoon of crushed fennel seed to a cup of boiling water and let it sit for 10 minutes.

- **Blackberries for diarrhoea!** Blackberries provide a remedy for dysentery and diarrhoea. Either eat them fresh, juice them or try pressing the blackberries into a juice. Add 1kg sugar for every 1.2 litres of the blackberry juice. Next, boil for five minutes, then allow to cool. You can keep this in the fridge and simply add water to this when you next feel the rumblings of thunder in your stomach.

- **Coffee for asthma!** Apparently, two cups of strong black coffee can help as an emergency measure in a mild asthma attack. There have been studies on this published in the *New England Journal of Medicine*. It keeps your airways open and allows you a bit more time to get hold of your medication or seek help.

- **Flaxseed to control food cravings!** Get hold of some quality flaxseed oil and add it to your salads, dressing or sprinkle on vegetables. Even better, sweeten it with manuka honey. Next, mix in some high quality unpasteurised vinegar which has also been shown to stifle appetite and prevent blood sugar spikes.

- **Black seed oil for fungal infections!** If you have athletes foot, nail infections or thrush, black seed may help. You can buy the extract in health stores and online as a topical ointment.

- **Cashews to reduce your hunger!** If you eat a cup of cashew nuts your stomach turns off hunger signals, thinking you've eaten a load of food. Now, there are quite a lot of calories in cashews, so consider just a handful when you feel hungry-it will stave off the need to eat for a little longer. If you want to be really healthy, cabbage does the same job and has barely any calories. So perhaps try juicing three cups worth of cabbage and using this as an appetite suppressant.

- **Ginkgo biloba for tinnitus!** According to some naturopaths this Asian herbal remedy can help relieve tinnitus. It's widely available in UK healthfood stores.

- **Oysters for BO!** According to some studies, many people with bad odour problems are deficient in zinc. Zinc-rich foods include oysters, liver, sardines, wholemeal bread, eggs and pumpkin seeds.

- **Eggs for dry skin!** According to Caroline Torres of *The New You Letter*, you should follow this recipe: Beat an egg in a bowl. Add half a cup of coconut oil and half a cup of honey, still beating as you go. When it's thick and creamy, pour it into an upright tube such as an empty toilet roll. Then put the tube in the freezer overnight. Peel back the tube and rub the stick on your face, like a giant lipbalm. Leave 10 minutes and rinse off.

Afterword

If you've enjoyed this book and haven't yet tried **The Good Life Letter**, please go to www.goodlifeletter.com and sign up. Twice every week I reveal breakthrough therapies and remedies for illnesses that most doctors write off as 'incurable'. I'll also show you natural ways to protect yourself against infection, age-related disease, stress and worry.

Here are some of the kinds of insight you'll get in **The Good Life Letter...**

- How nuts could help you lose weight, fight depression and heart disease, and even lower your levels of bad cholesterol.

- Why putting dill in your dinner could help relieve your irritable bowel syndrome.

- The Japanese diet secret that could help lower the chance of developing prostate disease.

- Why coffee could cure the morning blues and even boost your memory.

- How chilli peppers, cherries and peppermint could help relieve back pain.

- The amazing asthma remedy discovered in a Transylvanian mine.

You'll also discover how to lose weight without having to starve or give up many of the foods you love - like cheese, wine, red meat and chocolate.

Here's what other readers have said about The Good Life Letter...

"I have only very recently started to receive your letters but just wanted to say how much I am enjoying them, not only for their therapeutic content but for your obvious wit! I have laughed out loud a couple of times! That in itself is good for the health."
Shelagh Gibson

"I like your messages, they are full of great tips and wear me out just reading them and imagining the effort you put into them."
Joanne Phillips

"Thank you for yet another informative letter. I love the way you present these excellent nuggets in bite-size pieces with a twist of humour-very useful tool for getting a message across."
C.W.

"I would like to take the time to thank you for your wonderful down to earth emails."
Morag Craig

"As always you have produced another eye-opening Newsletter. How long will it be I wonder before the food manufactures club together and hire a Hit-man to silence you."
R.L.

It's really easy to sign up. Just go to www.goodlifeletter.com and enter your email details in the box on the top left. I'll do the rest.

This service is 100% free.
I'll never ask you to pay for *The Good Life Letter*.
And I'll never pass your email details to anyone else.

Index of Recipes

Index

More Great Books
by Ray Collins

The Lemon Book

Ray Collins reveals 76 amazing natural 'cure alls' for everyday problems

Ray Collins, author of The Spice Healer, has compiled 76 of the most astonishing ways the mighty lemon could help you and your family.

You'll be blown away by the many ways something as simple as a lemon could help you clean your home without toxins… repel insects… beautify your skin… relieve stress and dozens of niggling health problems… and even treat the symptoms of ageing!

The Lemon Book includes….

- How drinking this special lemon mixture 'through your nose' can beat asthma! Page 25
- Could a lemon cake mix keep you younger? Page 41
- Why on earth would you microwave a towel with lemons wrapped in it? Discover the answer on Page 44 (this could be the most powerful stress relief remedy EVER!)
- Get rid of cellulite for good. Just do this every day with a lemon! Page 26
- The sneaky lemon juice trick that boosts your baby's immune system. Page 26
- Got an interview or important meeting? Then you MUST do this with a lemon the night before (it involves fire, so be careful!) Page 27
- Constipation? Do this half an hour before you have breakfast. Page 27
- Over 60? The surprising reason why you should rub lemon juice on the back of your hands. Page 41
- If your kids suffer from nightmares, cut a lemon in half and use this simple trick on their feet! Page 32
- Blitz those spots with lemon juice and these two extra ingredients. Page 46
- Got sunburn? This lemon solution will soothe the pain, but you MUST mix the ingredients in these quantities. Page 34
- The amazing breakthrough of the "drunken" anti-wrinkle skin pack! Just mix lemon juice with this common tipple, and dab on your face. You won't believe the results. Page 42

To order The Lemon Book go to www.lemonbook.co.uk

The Honey, Garlic and Vinegar Miracle

129 Easy Ways to Lose Weight, Beat Disease and Feel Ten Years Younger

In this entertaining handbook, Ray Collins reveals how to clean your home the natural way... tackle dozens of everyday problems... and turn your kitchen cupboard into a natural pharmacy.

In The Honey, Garlic and Vinegar Miracle, he reveals:

- What you MUST take the minute anyone in your office, workplace or home picks up a flu bug.
- The BBC's amazing discovery about garlic and male impotence (the Chinese knew about this many centuries ago, this book reveals why).
- Why a report in The Lancet suggests this single ingredient could neutralise the effects of fatty food.
- Could a cabbage and this single ingredient really help reduce the appearance of wrinkles?
- How the ancient doctor Hippocrates solved his patients' eczema and skin problems (and an itch-relieving homemade recipe straight from your fridge!).
- Sleepless nights? Try this homemade syrup.
- The amazing true tale of how four thieves during a French plague protected themselves from disease and infection.
- A fast-healing and soothing idea for athlete's foot.
- Queen Anne's amazing home-made hair conditioner and other natural beauty treatments.
- How to make your own Vick's-style inhaler for a stuffy nose.
- What this New Zealand doctor has discovered about a very special type of honey and its potential benefits for indigestion, ulcers and wounds.
- How to create a homemade cough medicine to rival the pricy chemical-laden stuff in the shops.
- Allergy sufferers! Here are 12 natural ways to clean your home without using expensive, chemical irritants.
- What these 3 traditional foods could mean for joint pain sufferers.

To order, visit www.honeygarlicandvinegarmiracle.co.uk

Praise for Ray Collins

"I love the way you present these excellent nuggets in bite-size pieces with a twist of humour-very useful tool for getting a message across. Although I frequently read your missive and think "Yep, knew that" I also have lots of "Oooh, well I never" moments. Excellent." **C.W.**

"I find your e-mails sometimes very, very, very funny, but always interesting." **D.T.**

"Love reading your anecdotes and interesting health news, feel that you and your family are like the friends next door, and you make me laugh! I love your style of writing and good humour. Keep up the good work!" **M.D.**

"I am much obliged to you for these health notes, new breakthrough stuff and also the old ones which we can do with being reminded of." **M.M.**

"It's refreshing to see that common sense is not dead after all." **V.G.**

"Your letters are refreshingly easy to read and feel like you are a real person (which you are of course, doh!) but you are down to earth and give information that can be used and is easy for the normal everyday person to access the things you suggest." **L.P.**

"I read all your letters, they make me feel good, they give me a boost instead of feeling stuck in the mud" **L.M.**

"It's the way you write, it's just as if we are talking as old friends, I love it…" **B.A.**

"Your comments and tips (together with great humour) are a pleasure to receive and have proved most useful in my search for a reason (and answer) as to my health problems-which I hope are only temporary!" **M.B.**

"As time marches on, it is so necessary to take our health seriously and to do whatever we can to offset all the nasties which life throws at us." **J.D.**

"Thank you so much for sharing your wonderful knowledge and experiences with me. I have read each of these very interesting Good Life Letters in detail, some more than once and I am now building a healthy file of such valuable information." **Y.D.**

"Hugely helpful." **J.O.**

"Thank you very much for your interesting letters. They strike a real chord with me." **B.L.**

"I enjoy reading your letters. They are full of things that make absolute sense and jog your memory as to what you should be doing." **G.A.**

"Just to say thank you for your letter which I read with interest each time. You write a lot of common sense which I hope people will heed." **P.M.**

"I would like to say how interesting and informative your letters are. I am slowly compiling them into an indexed book, so that we have all your tips etc., at hand." **J.N.**

"Receiving your mail gives me a lift, and I find your topics very interesting." **H.R.**

"The information is really interesting. You have a great way of writing." **G.A.**

"I finally got my Honey, Garlic and Vinegar Miracle Book - thanks to you! I actually ordered another one for a friend. She is thrilled to bits." **Helen.**

"Thank you for this advice, it is particularly helpful as my mother was diagnosed with dementia two years ago. This has been very useful with some good tips for helping my mother and also to help prevent the same problem occurring with myself…" **L.B.**

"So informative on the natural way of relieving symptoms." **L.D.**

"Thank you for your letters, they are always informative and entertaining!" **S.B.**

"Your Good Life Letters are brilliant and very witty too!" **R.A.**

"May I take this opportunity of thanking you for such great and informative reading?" **W.C.**

"I enjoy your newsletter. It always has some really good and interesting information." **L.T.**

"I really enjoy reading your emails. I think you should do a column in a newspaper." **M.K.**

"Very interesting, amusing and entertaining all at once!!" **L.G.**

"I just wanted to say how much I am enjoying your letters and find them very informative. You put a lot of time, thought and effort into them and they are so interesting." **P.J.**

"I look forward to your letters, which are written with a smile." **Laura**

"I have just received my first edition of your Newsletter...brilliant!! At last, a newsletter where the author speaks English and in an interesting, amusing way. Congratulations, your newsletter is not only very informative-it is also brilliantly written and so very enjoyable." **Mrs Linda Morris.**

"Keep up the good work, always looking forward to receiving your emails they are full of good information which I have tried with good luck." **Norma Gianotti.**

"I just wanted to say I really appreciate your emails. They often make me laugh (good therapy in itself) and as I'm interested in all things to do with health, I find the content very interesting and relevant. I've also got a couple of your books and have put some of your advice into practice. So thanks and keep up the good work." **Steve.**

Notes

Notes

Notes

Notes

Notes

Notes

Notes

Notes

Notes

Notes

Notes